RED B

Wide Range
Readers

Phyllis Flowerdew

Oliver & Boyd

Illustrated by Gordon King

OLIVER & BOYD
Robert Stevenson House
1–3 Baxter's Place
Leith Walk
Edinburgh EH1 3BB
A Division of Longman Group Ltd

First published 1982
Second impression 1983

ISBN 0 05 003082 5

Printed in Hong Kong by
Wing King Tong Printing Co., Ltd.

Preface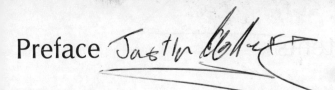

There are eight Wide Range Readers Red Books. Books 1–6 can be used alone or with Wide Range Readers Blue and Green, with which they are parallel, and Books 7 and 8 follow on from the Book 6 level. The controlled vocabulary of Books 1–6 makes them suitable for children with the following reading ages:

7 to $7\frac{1}{2}$ years	– Book 1
$7\frac{1}{2}$ to 8 years	– Book 2
8 to $8\frac{1}{2}$ years	– Book 3
$8\frac{1}{2}$ to 9 years	– Book 4
9 to 10 years	– Book 5
10 to 11 + years	– Book 6

Books 7 and 8 are necessarily more loosely controlled but are broadly suitable for reading ages 11 to 12 and 12 to 13. Their subject matter is parallel to the Book 6 level and Books 7 and 8 are therefore suitable for children needing further graded reading practice before transferring completely to independent reading.

Contents

Sister Coler

The Long Act

Atilio was a lion tamer. His act always took just twenty minutes. He was confident but careful. Never did he take his eyes off the lions. Never for a moment did he let his concentration falter. Never – until tonight . . . .

His name, of course, was not Atilio. It was plain Mr Reginald Borg. He was the owner of the circus, and for his own act he had three lions and a lioness. Jupiter, the leader of the group, was big and powerful, with a great shaggy mane standing up like a sandy halo round his head. He had not been easy to train, and behind the passive submission was a smouldering fire of ferocity. Atilio was well aware of this and he felt all the more proud of the fact that he had subdued Jupiter and received, he thought, a sort of affection from him. Sheba, the lioness, was a quiet, lovable

creature, resigned to a life of cage bars, all she had ever remembered. The other two lions, Luke and Leo, were young, unrelated males, fully grown but still playful, mischievous, reasonably tolerant, and ready to follow Jupiter and Sheba in the somewhat stupid actions they were expected to perform.

Atilio had a daughter of fifteen called Suzi. She had grown up in the circus, taking part happily in all the daily activities, except the actual performances. From babyhood she had ridden on elephants, leaped on to horses, fondled sea-lions, exercised poodles, played with chimpanzees. This morning in the caravan, drinking coffee, Atilio had felt it a good moment to say,

"Well Suzi, it's time you became a paid member of the troupe. Have you decided what you're going to make your special act?"

She shrugged her shoulders, as if not very interested. She had become thoughtful and withdrawn of late, so that her father sometimes felt an almost imperceptible barrier rising between her and himself – just the process of growing up, he supposed. He tried again.

"Suzi, you're pretty capable with all the animals. What will be your career?" She hesitated a moment and then said firmly,

"I don't intend to go into the circus." He thought he must have misheard her.

"What did you say?" he asked in disbelief.

"I don't want a career in the circus," she said. She felt a wave of pity for her father. She was fond of him and didn't want to hurt him. He had always taken it for granted that she would join him in the circus one day. She knew this must be a terrible blow to him.

"But your mother, your grandfather –" he began.

"Yes, I know," she interrupted, "and great-grandfather. Our family have all been circus people, but I'm different."

"But why, Suzi, why?"

"Because I don't agree with circuses," she said.

"Don't agree with them! What do you mean? The circus is our whole life. How can you suddenly say you don't agree with it?"

"It's the animals. I don't agree with performing animals."

"But they're happy. They don't know any other life. We are kind to them."

"Yes I know, but it's wrong all the same. It's unnatural. It's undignified. It's wrong to make a living by making animals do unnatural things. They can't argue or protest. Just think of Charlie and his Chimps – clever, wild animals wearing ridiculous clothes and riding on silly little bicycles – and your lions, Daddy –

7

strong, noble creatures standing on their back legs at your command or perching on little wooden drums. It's so wrong."

"Oh Suzi, you're being silly and sentimental." Someone knocked on the caravan door and the conversation ended abruptly.

Now it was evening. The lights were ablaze and the circus was well under way. A much-painted lady called Angela was sending her troupe of poodles jumping through hoops and climbing on to seesaws. Atilio was watching from the ringside. He saw the act now as Suzi would see it. It was unnatural and ridiculous, but the audience loved it. Why deprive people of their enjoyment?

It was the turn of the clowns now, and then it would be his own act – Atilio the Lion Tamer. He was tense and nervous as he always was before he entered the ring. The people were laughing as the clowns ran and tumbled and shouted and performed their age-old tricks with ladders and buckets of water. Then, amid the laughter, there was a sudden hush followed by a hundred half-stifled exclamations of awe and anticipation as a group of odd-job men began carrying the lions' railings into the ring.

"Oh, the lions next," murmured the audience, and they hardly noticed the clumsy, amusing departure of the clowns for they were watching the men assembling the lions' railings with swift movements and noisy clangings. In a few moments the cage was ready. The covered, railed walkway was put in position, but before the gap was closed, Atilio entered the cage to receive the lions. There was the usual pause while he stood proudly and bowed to this side and that. Atilio the Lion Tamer! The crowd greeted him with a thunder of clapping. The lion tamer was always the most popular act. How could Suzi say it was wrong when the crowd loved it so? A feeling of worry and bitter disappointment lingered in Atilio's mind. He must dismiss it. The lions were ambling up the enclosed walkway. He must concentrate.

Jupiter entered the arena, big, powerful and splendid with his great shaggy mane standing up like a sandy halo round his head. There was a glint in his eye and a look, surely, of disdain. He padded round in the expected way, followed by Sheba. Sheba was quiet as always but Luke and Leo, the two young lions, seemed inattentive and playful and appeared to be amusing themselves over a private joke.

Atilio's orders were quiet and forceful. First the animals were to stand on the small wooden drums, their feet close together, a somewhat unnatural position for the king of beasts. Jupiter appeared to refuse at first with an angry-looking snarl. This was a rehearsed part of the act. It looked a dangerous situation and added to the tension and excitement of the audience. In actual fact, Jupiter behaved in an exemplary manner. Sheba followed him, and Luke and Leo quietened down and did all they were expected to do.

Atilio relaxed and put Suzi out of his mind. He was filled as always with a glorious sense of power and happiness. The lions performed perfectly. The audience was silent, tense, thrilled, identifying themselves with Atilio every step of the way. Atilio the Lion Tamer! He was proud. He was happy.

The time seemed to pass in a flash. Now for the grand finale – the moment when the lions would take up their positions on a step ladder. Luke was the main star here. He balanced himself on the top, while Jupiter and Sheba stood on each side, their back paws on the lowest steps, their front paws three-quarters of the way up. Leo placed himself like a friendly kitten underneath the ladder, at the base of the pyramid.

Atilio looked at them with pride.

"What splendid, handsome creatures they are," he thought. Then suddenly, Suzi's words came back to him.

"It's unnatural. It's undignified," and in that moment he visualised the lions as they should be, padding through the African bush, living their lives uninfluenced by man, proud, beautiful creatures, wild and free. In that moment he knew that Suzi was right, and that he and the circus and his whole livelihood were wrong.

He stood motionless, a moment longer than usual. Jupiter noticed the delay and made an impatient movement. Luke took it as a sign to dismount, almost pushing the bigger lion out of the way. Atilio was jerked back into reality. For a brief moment he had lost concentration and in that moment the routine of years had been broken. Instead of each lion stepping down lightly in turn, at his command, the descent had become a shambles. The twenty minutes was up. The odd-job men were sliding aside the clanking rail that separated the cage from the iron-railed walkway.

Atilio felt ashamed. The grand finale was spoiled and he had only himself to blame. All he could do now was to get the lions out of the ring as gracefully as possible.

"Out!" he said to Jupiter, but Jupiter had already passed the exit and was walking round again. Sheba followed him and Luke and Leo fell in behind her. Silently they padded round until they reached the exit again.

"Out!" commanded Atilio, but Jupiter plodded on past the exit once more, as if the order had not been for him at all. Behind him in single file went Sheba, Luke and Leo. Twice they passed the exit, three times, four times.

"Out!" shouted Atilio. He was trembling now. He had lost control of the lions. Their routine had been broken and they were going their own way. Temporarily his power over them had gone. Somehow he had to get it back. With all the force of his mind, he willed Jupiter to obey as he reached the exit again.

"Out!" he cried, but his voice was husky, and the big lion knew that he was afraid. Atilio saw the white, scared faces of the odd-job men as they waited for the lions to enter the walkway so that they could dismantle the cage. Two of them had iron bars in their hands ready to use against the animals if necessary. They knew Atilio had lost control. They knew there was danger, yet they hesitated to intervene in case they brought disaster upon him.

"Out!" screamed Atilio. "Out, Jupiter, out!" He was wet with perspiration and weak with fear. It was

like a nightmare, going on and on and on, as the lions padded ceaselessly round the cage, ignoring the exit every time.

At first the audience had thought the whole affair was part of the prepared performance, but by this time they were well aware that Atilio had become a helpless puppet and that the lions were refusing to leave the ring. The people were thrilled and horrified and the silence in the big top was so intense that it could almost be heard. Meanwhile the lions padded on and on. By how many minutes had the act over-run its time? Three, five, ten, fifteen? To Atilio it seemed an eternity.

He made a supreme effort to shake off his fear. He had the sudden idea of trying to persuade Jupiter to start the act again – to stand on his wooden drum as if the performance were just beginning – anything to break the relentless cycle of passing and passing and passing the exit.

"Jupiter!" he cried with all the authority his weary voice could muster, "Jupiter! Up!" For a second the great lion paused. He was puzzled and angry and frustrated and he knew it was not time to stand on the drum.

Atilio realised at once that his plan was not going to work. His mouth was dry with fear, and perspiration was running down his forehead into his eyes.

"Jupiter! Out!" he cried and the next moment the great beast was upon him, its mighty paws pressing into his chest, its snarling jaws close to his face. He heard a united gasp of horror from the audience and the clanging of iron as the odd-job men tried to attack the lion through the bars of the cage. Then he knew no more.

A few days later, Suzi came to visit her father in hospital. It was the first time he had felt well enough to notice anything around him, and he was filled with pleasure because he was beginning to recover from the lion's attack.

"Oh, you're looking much better today," said Suzi in relief as she sat on a chair beside his bed.

"Suzi," he said. "You were right about performing animals. I had come to that conclusion before Jupiter attacked me. The circus has been my life, but I'll have to think again."

"I've been thinking about it too," said Suzi. "You know, you could have a grand circus without using animals at all. You could just have people – trapeze artists, jugglers, acrobats, clowns. You could advertise it as a circus without animals. And think of the money you'd save on food and transport for animals. I'm sure it could be a good circus. Think of it, Daddy – "The Circus Without Animals!"

Atilio nodded.

"Maybe we *could* do something like that," he agreed. "It might prove to be quite a good idea." He paused, then asked, "What happened to Jupiter?"

"One of the men shot him. It was Ben. It was clever of him to do it without hitting you. That's another act you could have – someone shooting at five-pound notes and such things. There are all sorts of exciting possibilities."

"Mm." Atilio nodded. Then he said, "The act went on so long, so long. I thought it would never end."

"I thought so too," smiled Suzi.

"How long over time was it?"

"Only four minutes, I think."

"Impossible, impossible." Atilio laughed. Then he sank back on his pillow, tired, but not too unhappy. Atilio the Lion Tamer had gone for ever. He became Mr Reginald Borg again, and Mr Reginald Borg would build up one of the best of travelling circuses, "The Circus Without Animals".

The Story of Gideon

It is thought that part of the story of Gideon was lost and that the rather confused narrative in the Old Testament is a mixture of two separate accounts. It remains however a stirring story of an ordinary man rising up to deliver his people from oppression. It has the added interest of little chats with God and of decisions confirmed by visible signs and wonders.

For many years the Israelites had been attacked and harassed by various desert tribes, particularly the Midianites. The Midianites had come like swarms of locusts upon the land. They had stolen cattle and sheep. They had destroyed the harvests. They had dominated life in Israel for seven years. They were hated and feared.

One harvest time a man named Gideon was threshing wheat at the back of a winepress beneath an oak tree, hoping to complete the work quickly before any Midianites should notice him. Then the voice of God came to him – either as a thought in his mind or as a message from a heavenly visitor in the guise of a man.

"Go forth, Gideon, and save the land of Israel from the oppression of the Midianites. I the Lord will be with you."

"Oh Lord!" said Gideon. "How can I save Israel? My family is poor, and I am the poorest of my family."

"Go forth," repeated the Lord, "and you shall overcome the Midianites as if they were only one man. I will be with you."

"But how can I tell that your voice is really that of the Lord?" asked Gideon, knowing well that it might be his own imagination or a half-remembered dream. "Please give me a sign to prove that you have been talking to me. Meanwhile, wait a little and I will bring an offering to you." He hurried into his house and brought out a basket of goat flesh and some little cakes and a pot of broth. He placed them on the ground beneath the oak tree and said,

"Here, Lord, is my offering."

Then the voice came again, saying,

"Put the goat flesh and the little cakes upon this

rock and pour out the broth." Gideon obeyed, and at once a fire rose out of the rocks and consumed the goat flesh and the little cakes and dried up the broth.

Then Gideon believed that the Lord had indeed been talking with him. (Later he built an altar in that place, which remained there for many years.) Even so, he was still not convinced that he could save Israel and he asked for a further sign, saying,

"Oh Lord, if you will really enable me to save Israel, give me a sign. I will put a fleece of wool on the ground and leave it there all night. If, in the morning, I find that the ground is quite dry but the fleece is wet with dew, then I shall know that you will give me power to save Israel, as you have said."

So that evening Gideon spread a fleece on the ground and left it there all night. He rose early the next morning and found that the earth was quite dry but the fleece was soaked with dew. It was so wet that he wrung and twisted it in his hands and squeezed out a bowl full of water.

This was the sign he had asked for, but still his confidence was lacking.

"Oh Lord," he said apologetically, "don't be angry with me, but just give me one more sign to show that you will enable me to save Israel, as you have said. I will leave the fleece on the ground again tonight.

If, in the morning, I find it is quite dry but that the earth is wet with dew, then I shall know that you will give me power to save Israel."

So again in the evening, Gideon spread the fleece on the ground and left it there all night. He rose early in the morning and went to look at it, half hoping that the sign might have failed and that he would not be called upon to undertake such a tremendous task. But no – the ground was wet with dew and only the fleece was dry. There was no excuse for him not to act. He had received three signs – the fire on the rock, the wet fleece on the dry ground and the dry fleece on the wet ground. He could not ask for more.

He called the people together and led them to a camp beside the well of Harod, so that the Midianites were in the valley on the north side of them. The Israelites were glad to have a leader to rally round and they awaited his orders with enthusiasm. But first the Lord had something to say to Gideon.

"There are too many people with you. If they drive the Midianites out of Israel they will be puffed up with pride and declare that they have saved themselves. They will give no credit to you or to me. You must reduce the size of the army."

"Lord, how can I do that, when the men are all so keen?"

"They are not all so keen. Some are afraid and some are already wishing that they had not come. Go to them and say, 'Those who are fearful or afraid, let them leave!'"

So Gideon stood up before the great crowd of people spreading over the hill beside the well of Harod.

"We do not need so great an army," he declared. "If any of you are nervous therefore and would rather not take part, you are free to leave now." Some looked at each other furtively and slipped quietly away. Others walked boldly and gladly back to their homes. Many left, but ten thousand remained.

"There are still too many," said the Lord to Gideon. "You must reduce the number still further."

"But these are the brave ones, the strong ones," protested Gideon. "How can I decide which of them are to leave and which to stay?"

"Lead them down to the water and tell them to drink," explained the Lord. "Watch them carefully. Some will kneel down and bow their heads over the water and drink it in gulps. Others will raise water to their lips in their hands and lap it with their tongues as a dog laps. Separate them according to the way they drink."

So Gideon led the ten thousand to the water and asked them to drink. Three hundred of them raised water to their lips in their hands and lapped it with their tongues as a dog laps. Three hundred did this, but all the rest knelt down and bowed their heads over the water and gulped.

"By the three hundred men that lapped, I will save you," said the Lord to Gideon. "These three hundred are the good soldiers, the alert, the watchful ones. These shall form your army."

So the three hundred camped that night on the hillside, and the hosts of Midian camped below them in the valley. Great were the hosts of Midian, lying in their tents like a multitude of grasshoppers. Great too were the numbers of their camels, as many it seemed as the grains of sand by the sea. It was no wonder that Gideon still had qualms of fear, so that the Lord deemed it necessary to strengthen his courage.

"Creep down among the enemy tents," he said, "and listen to what the men say, for with my help you will overcome them this night."

So Gideon crept down into the valley and walked among the enemy's tents. Then he heard one of the Midianites say to another,

"I've just been dreaming. I dreamed that a cake of barley bread came tumbling on to one of our tents and overturned it."

"A strange thing to dream," said his companion. "It must mean that Gideon the Israelite will conquer us, the Midianites."

When Gideon heard this, his spirits were lifted and he crept back up the hillside to his own men, confident at last that the Lord would deliver the Midianites into his hand.

Quietly he gathered his army round him and to each man he gave a trumpet, a pitcher and a lamp.

"We shall surround the camp of the Midianites in the silence of the middle watch," he said. "When you hear me blow my trumpet, you will all blow yours. At the same time you will smash your pitchers and hold up your lamps and shout, 'The sword of the Lord and of Gideon!'"

So the three hundred men of the army of Israel crept down into the valley and surrounded the camp of the Midianites in the silence of the middle watch. Suddenly the Midianites were awakened by a single trumpet note, followed at once by the blaring of three hundred trumpets and the crashing of breaking pitchers and the flashing of lamps and the shouting of the Israelites,

"The sword of the Lord and of Gideon!"

In the camp, all was fear and confusion. Taken by surprise the Midianites scattered and fled in panic and the Israelites pursued them in triumph.

Liberated at last, the people of Israel turned to Gideon in gratitude and begged him to become their king.

"Rule over us," they said. "Be our king, and let your son follow in your footsteps, and let your son's son rule us in his turn."

"No," replied Gideon. "I will not rule over you. Nor shall my son, nor my son's son. Only the Lord shall rule over you."

So the Midianites were driven from the land, and the people of Israel lived in peace for forty years. Gideon meanwhile grew to be an old man. He took many wives, as was the custom of the time, and he fathered many, many children.

The Biography of a Horse

He was born in Virginia on a cold February night. The birth of a foal at any time must look like a miracle – the appearance of the damp, sleek muzzle and the long, stiff front legs – then ten or twenty minutes later, the bedraggled little body and back legs in their membrane sac, sliding on to the straw of the stable floor – a complete and perfect young horse.

This one rested a little after the exertions of entering the world. Then in an unbelievably short time, he was trying out his awkward-looking legs and standing beside his mother, taking milk from her. Probably he was considered especially beautiful from the first. He had a bright, reddish-brown coat. He came from a long line of race horses, and great hopes were pinned on him from the moment of his birth.

He belonged to Mr Paul Mellon, who bred race horses in America, and who had horses in England too. He called this foal Mill Reef after an area of coastline near his home. His Virginian stud was very large, with stables and stable yards and huge areas of grassland, with maple and sycamore woods and gum trees and oaks and flowing streams. This was to be Mill Reef's home for almost two years. For the first year he lived a pleasantly ordered life, playing in the fields with other young horses or allowing himself to be led and exercised.

When he was a year old he was introduced to a saddle and a lightweight rider. Some young horses object to the feel of a saddle and the burden of a rider but Mill Reef accepted them without any trouble at all. He had a beautiful, easy movement, a promise of great speed. He seemed to have the right sort of temperament for a racer. He was full of nervous energy. He had courage and stamina. He learned quickly and responded well to training.

In America, race tracks are made of hard earth, but in England they are of soft, springy, green turf. Mill Reef, with his slender legs, had a very light footfall, and it was thought that he would probably be faster on grass than on dirt. So when he was nearly two years old he was taken to England to a place called Kingsclere.

Race horses are cherished and cared for in every respect and Mill Reef quickly settled down to his new surroundings. The air was crisper, colder than it had been in Virginia. The grass was softer, greener. He was introduced to Ian Balding, his trainer, and to John Hallum, the stable man who was to look after him for years to come. Mill Reef galloped over the downs, his

reddish-brown coat gleaming, his small hooves leaving scarcely a footprint behind. He had a wonderful flowing movement and a most impressive speed. He was a fine horse. He was full of promise.

He won his first real race at Salisbury as a two-year-old and a month later he ran at Royal Ascot. He stood in the starting stalls waiting to begin. When the doors opened in front of him, he knew he was expected to run. There was no casual trot for Mill Reef. He simply shot out like a bullet from a gun and

found himself ahead of the other horses at the very start of the race. He drew further and further ahead, galloping so fast that his jockey could not stop him at the winning post, but had to let him run on till he could slow him down. This famous race was a real triumph. Mill Reef as a two-year-old had made his name.

Race horses are so highly bred that they are often extremely nervous. They twitch anxiously at sudden movements near them. They prick up their ears at unusual sounds. They start fearfully at unexpected sights – an umbrella opening perhaps or a big results board towering ahead. Mill Reef had a lot of things to get used to as the racing season advanced. Sometimes, too, there were long journeys to be taken in horse boxes to racing tracks. These could be tiring and upsetting and for Mill Reef they could be boring, for he liked company. When John Hallum noticed that he was becoming restless, he or one of the men would travel in the horse box with him, talking to him and keeping him happy.

Mill Reef came second in a race in July and won one in August. He came first at Newmarket in October and first at Newbury the next April. Winter meanwhile was a time of rest, of gentle gallops on the downs and rolling joyfully in the sandpits. He was growing in size and strength and he needed plenty of food – with a daily menu as follows:

Breakfast	1 kilogram of dry oats.
Lunch	3 kilograms of oats. 2 handfuls of bran and chaff, or grass or chopped dandelions (very tasty these).
Supper	4 kilograms of oats, plus chaff, bran or grass. 6 shelled eggs. $\frac{1}{4}$ kilogram of honey.
Night-time snack	1 kilogram of dry oats.

Winters were pleasant enough, but Mill Reef preferred work to rest. He seemed to love extending himself to the full, running against other fast horses, overtaking them, galloping ahead, leading the field in all the excitement of the racing season.

When he was three years old he was entered for the Derby, the most famous of all British races. It is held in June, on Epsom Downs. Usually a fair sets up its dodgem cars and roundabouts on the edge of the grass, and gypsies park their caravans there a few days before. On Derby Day itself the Downs become a restless sea of cars and people, with the spectator stands holding only a small fraction of those who want to watch the race. People jostle and chatter and push. Bookmakers shout. Gypsies thread their way in and out, trying to sell their tiny sprigs of "lucky white heather" and offering to "tell your fortune, lady". Traffic jams on the approach roads are so great that cars can be delayed for hours. Mill Reef, therefore, left home very early in his horsebox, led by a security van. Then he was able to wait quietly in the Epsom stables, out of sight and sound of the maelstrom of traffic and people.

It was a hot sunny day. When it was time for Mill Reef to canter past the stands, people who had watched his progress over the year noticed that he was now a heavier, stronger horse, with firm, rippling muscles beneath his handsome red-brown coat. The race was two and a half kilometres, the longest Mill Reef had attempted. Would he be able to keep up his speed? Would he be able to put on the necessary extra spurt at the end? Everyone would soon know now.

The first part of the race was uphill. Mill Reef rushed out of the starting stalls, tossed his head and swung into action. Swiftly he passed one horse after another until only three were left to offer him a serious challenge. Then there was only one, a horse called Linden Tree, who struggled to stay ahead. He nearly managed it, but Mill Reef was not going to allow this. He put forth every bit of his strength and stamina and determination. He overtook Linden Tree and ran neck and neck with him. Another spurt and he had passed him. Another spurt and he had gained two lengths and won the Derby. This achievement, for race-horse owners and for trainers and jockeys, is the most coveted triumph in the world. To win the Derby! It is the dream of hundreds.

In the evening Mill Reef travelled back in the horse-box to his stable at Kingsclere. The villagers had hung flags from the houses and strung bunting and coloured

streamers across the road to welcome him. Mill Reef was led out of the box to accept their greetings and their praise. He was tired, but patiently he allowed men, women and numerous children to pat him and stroke him and murmur his name – Mill Reef, the Derby winner.

There were other races and other successes, and there were hopes that Mill Reef might win the Prix de l'Arc de Triomphe in France in October. He was a very valuable horse these days. At Kingsclere a burglar alarm was fixed to the stables and a policeman with a dog guarded them at night. When he took the Channel flight to France, Mill Reef was insured for two million pounds. There were the usual worries about the journey and about the horse's condition, but Mill Reef ran well, among a bunch of other horses also running well. He galloped swiftly and bravely as always. Then, near the end, he had a sudden moment of luck when a gap appeared between the contestants, enabling him to burst through and gallop triumphantly to the winning post – the first English horse to win this race for twenty-three years.

Another restful winter passed at Kingsclere, and spring came again, with other races. Mill Reef was a four-year-old now, and the plans made for his races against other powerful four-year-olds were arousing much anticipation and excitement. Most thrilling of all, people thought, would be the next Prix de l'Arc de Triomphe in France, and Mill Reef's training was continued with this race particularly in mind. He was regarded as one of the greatest race horses of the quarter century, and he was expected to continue his brilliant career for a long time to come.

Then one day at the end of August he was enjoying his morning gallop with John Hallum on his back, when there was the sound of a sudden, loud, frightening crack. One of Mill Reef's front legs seemed to go out of action, and John Hallum was tipped forward on to the horse's mane. An unthinkable disaster had happened. Four bones in Mill Reef's left foreleg were broken, and splintered fragments were already slipping out of place to cause further complications. Mill Reef's career as a racing horse had come to a sudden and dramatic end. Never would he race again. It was doubtful whether he would even live.

A horse with a broken leg is a tragic creature. Its great body cannot easily be supported on only three legs and it is almost impossible for it to lie down in any comfort – or, if lying down, ever to get up again. It has, in fact, in the past, been the sad policy to destroy such injured animals. Mill Reef, however, was to be given the very best of care and veterinary surgery. A big, airy room at the stables was converted to a hospital. After an x-ray he was given an anaesthetic, and the surgeon performed a seven-hour operation on his leg. He removed the fragments of bone and screwed a supporting plate into place. Then he encased the whole of the leg in plaster, strengthened with an iron splint. The men stacked bales of straw round the horse to make a comfortable nest for him, and an hour after the completion of the operation Mill Reef regained consciousness.

Anxious days followed. Unable to take his normal food, Mill Reef was given vitamin injections and glucose drips. Ian Balding and John Hallum and volunteer stable boys took turns to watch over him day and night. His hospital room was decorated with five hundred "get well" cards, sent by his admirers, some of whom had read about his accident in the papers, or had seen him only on television. He also received

letters and gifts including sugar lumps and pepper-
mints and all sorts of sweets and candies, which he and
the stable boys much appreciated. Many people sent
him money, far too much for his needs, so Ian Balding
kindly spent some of it on a fine rocking horse for a
local children's home. It was, of course, christened
Mill Reef.

With the devoted care of the Kingsclere staff, and
with his own patience and courage, Mill Reef slowly
recovered. Forty days after the operation, the plaster
was taken off his leg, and the surgeon found that the
broken bones had healed and knitted together again.
Now came the difficult task for Mill Reef of daring to
put his foot to the ground and trying to use the leg
again. He had grown rather thin, and though he learned
to walk and even, with encouragement, to trot a little,
it seemed doubtful whether he would ever be brave
enough to attempt a gallop.

Then one day, while he was grazing unsaddled in a field, a shout nearby frightened him. To the delight of the staff he shot forward as if he were taking part in a race. He galloped across the field on his four slender legs, scarcely limping at all.

His racing days of course were over, but he went now to live at the National Stud at Newmarket. There over the years he fathered many foals, some of whom would inherit his gentle, brave temperament and his incredible powers of speed, some who, one day, might win the English Derby or the French Prix de l'Arc de Triomphe.

The facts in this story were taken from the book *The Story of Mill Reef* by John Oaksey, published by Michael Joseph.

The Strange Story of Anne Jefferies

In these days we do not pour scorn on people who believe there is life on other planets, so it is quite easy to understand that for hundreds of years many people believed most firmly in fairies. After all, strange things happened from time to time. Things appeared or disappeared. Bad luck dogged some families. Good luck came to others. There were good harvests and bad harvests. Things were mysteriously broken. It seemed quite reasonable to give credit or blame to the Little People, as they were usually called. All the same, a girl named Anne Jefferies, who lived in Cornwall in the seventeenth century, brought quite a bit of trouble upon herself by becoming too familiar with them (or more likely by using her imagination too freely).

She was a brave, bright girl, the daughter of a poor labourer. She was intensely curious about fairies and spent many a summer evening turning up fern leaves and peering into foxgloves in search of them. When she was nineteen she went to live as a servant at the home of Mr Moses Pitt. One day when she had finished her work, she was sitting in his garden knitting when she heard the click of the gate accompanied by a rustling in the bushes and the sound of suppressed laughter. Thinking it was her boy friend, she pretended not to notice, but when no one appeared she said a little crossly,

"You may stay there till mildew grows on the gate before I'll come to you."

Then there was a tinkling sound and a most musical laugh that certainly did not belong to any of Anne's acquaintances. She felt a little afraid but she stayed where she was and waited.

Then (so she declared afterwards), six little men came into the garden and looked so kindly upon her that she lost her fear at once. They were all dressed in green and they were so small that they were able to climb over her and touch her hair, her cheeks, her lips, her eyes. When her eyes were touched they felt as if they had been pricked with a pin. At that moment everything became dark and she was whirled swiftly through the air.

When she landed she found herself in a most beautiful place where everything was sunny and bright. There were (so she said afterwards) wonderful temples and palaces. There were trees laden with luscious fruit and fields full of brilliant flowers. There were gold and silver fish swimming in cool blue lakes and the air was filled with the song of birds. Many people were strolling about the gardens or sitting in the leafy arbours. They were all most beautifully dressed and there was no longer any difference in size between Anne and her six fairy gentlemen and all the other people. After a while one of the six men in green led

Anne away to a quiet corner where they chatted happily for some time. Never had Anne been anywhere so beautiful or felt so blissfully content. She would gladly have stayed here for ever, but suddenly the other five green men burst in upon them, followed by a noisy crowd.

Again Anne found herself whirling through the air in darkness. There was a great humming sound as if a thousand insects were buzzing around her. Then her eyes opened to daylight and she found that she was lying on the ground in Mr Moses Pitt's garden where she had been before. Friends were standing anxiously

round her, assuming that she was recovering from convulsions or a sudden illness of some kind. She was carried into Mr Pitt's house, put to bed and looked after until she recovered her strength. However, though she resumed her previous mode of life, things were never to be quite the same again.

She told her friends about her experiences. Some of them believed her and some did not, but the news spread through the countryside and beyond, especially as she now began to utter prophecies and to heal the sick. This was due to powers that the fairies had given her, she said. In a letter written many years later by Moses Pitt's son (also named Moses Pitt), to the Bishop of Gloucester, he said,

"People of all distempers, sickness, sores and agues, came not only so far as the Land's End but also from London, and were cured by her. She took no moneys of them nor any reward that I ever knew or heard of, yet had she moneys at all times to supply her wants. She neither made nor bought any medicines or salves that ever I saw or heard of, yet wanted them not as she had occasion. She forsook eating our victuals, and was fed by the fairies from that harvest time till the next Christmas Day; upon which day she came to our table and said, because it was that day, she would eat some roast beef with us, the which she did – I myself being then at the table."

He told too, how on one occasion she gave him a piece of her fairy bread, "which I did eat, and I think it was the most delicious bread that ever I did eat, either before or since."

News of this unusual young woman came eventually

to the ears of Mr John Tregeagle, a severe and un-imaginative justice of the peace, and he sent a constable to arrest her. According to Anne's account, the fairies warned her of his coming.

"Shall I hide myself?" she asked.

"No," they replied. "Fear nothing, but go with the constable." So when the constable came for her, she went with him to the court of Justice Tregeagle who committed her to Bodmin Jail, giving orders to the prison-keeper that she should not be given any food.

She was kept in prison for some time, and after that she was confined to Tregeagle's house. During all this time she was given no food. Yet she lived and remained in good health, being fed, it was said, by the fairies.

Eventually she was released. She went into service again, near the town of Padstow, and after a while she married a man called William Warren, with whom it is hoped she lived happily ever after. In 1693, when she was about sixty-seven years of age, she was visited by Mr Humphrey Martin, an old friend of the Pitts. He spent nearly a whole day with her, but with vivid memories of Justice Tregeagle's unkindness, she refused to acknowledge any of the stories told about her.

"Why won't you tell me of your youthful experiences?" Mr Martin asked kindly.

"Because if I were to tell you, you would make books or ballads about it," she replied, "and I will not have my name spread about the country in books or ballads – not even for five hundred pounds."

Poor Anne! No doubt she was wise to remain silent and to keep her memories or her delusions to herself. When she had been nineteen and full of imagination and enthusiasm, the year had been 1645. If she had been alive today, might she not have seen Unidentified Flying Objects, and would not her little green men have come from Mars instead of Fairyland?

David Douglas

Searching for unusual plants sounds a quiet and peaceful occupation, but behind many of the flowers that bloom in our gardens today are stories of bravery, danger and disaster. Here is one:

David Douglas was born at Scone, where in years gone by Scottish kings had been crowned. He was an awkward, humourless and aggressive child, a trial to his parents, and a disruptive influence in the village school. He appeared to be lazy, but probably that was because he was not interested in the subjects that were taught at that time. He *was* interested, however, in plants and flowers and trees. He was delighted therefore, when, at the tender age of ten, his father suggested that he should leave school and start an apprenticeship as a gardener's boy.

His father had a friend, William Beattie, who was head gardener at a huge mansion nearby, and it was here that David went willingly to learn and work. The large grounds with their stately trees, their brilliant flower beds and their neat vegetable plots gave him a glimpse of paradise. He was perfectly happy digging, weeding, watering, transplanting, pollinating. He worked hard for long hours and he also became interested in reading. He read natural history books and travel books, which opened his eyes to the fact that there must be hundreds of flowers that had never been seen here in Scotland. The idea came to him that one day he might save enough money to go to foreign lands and search for foreign plants.

When he was eighteen and his apprenticeship finished, he procured a job in an even bigger and more exotic garden, and two years later he became a member of the staff of the Botanical Garden at Glasgow. Here his interest and skill were noticed by Professor Hooker of the university and when, a few years later, the London Horticultural Society was looking for someone to collect plants in America, David Douglas was considered to be just the man. So at the age of twenty-four he began a life of travel and adventure.

In those days, much of America and Canada was unmapped. It was wild, unexplored land where often no man had trod. In many places the only people were Indians, sometimes friendly but sometimes hostile. For more than three years, David Douglas experienced unimaginable difficulties and hardships. He travelled great distances on foot, or on snowshoes. He swam across icy rivers and went through terrifying storms when giant trees crashed to earth around him, and lightning tore jaggedly at his courage. In such weather his nightly camp fire would not burn and his tent blew away.

He was plagued by ants and by rats which ate some of the seeds he had collected. Sometimes he was so hungry that he ate the seeds and roots himself. He battled with snow drifts and avalanches and wounds and fevers. Twice he lost his precious collections. Twice he met grizzly bears. Sometimes he was able to make journeys on horseback and sometimes down long stretches of river by canoe. There he survived storms and bitter cold, and his canoe eventually was broken to pieces by angry water.

Being a man of short temper and no great patience even in comfortable circumstances, it is surprising that he did not give up the struggle, but he was willing to suffer anything for plants, and he was driven on and on by his determination and enthusiasm. Certainly he had results too. In spite of all disasters, he shipped back cases full of seeds and cones to Britain. He took back pages of notes on unusual plants and unusual animals. He told stories of gigantic trees – more than sixty metres high – Sugar Pines and the tall, tall trees now called after him – Douglas Firs.

Back at last in Britain, he was praised and heaped with honours. He could have led an easy, carefree life in London society, basking in admiration and approval – but this was not for him. He was restless, impatient, irritable. He longed to go back to the wilderness and search for more of his beloved plants. He had a few good friends, but he did not fit at all well into civilised life, and it was at this time that he adopted a little black Scottish terrier called Billy, who became his constant and much-loved companion. David Douglas quarrelled with many people but he never quarrelled with Billy, and when he left Britain again in 1829 the faithful little dog went with him.

This time his expeditions led him to California and Columbia. There he collected animals, insects and birds for the London Zoological Society, and seeds and scores of new plants for the Horticultural Society. He expcrienced the usual discomforts and hair-breadth escapes. Somehow he avoided a terrible fever that wiped out hundreds of Indians. Somehow he survived more than an hour and a half of swirling round in a whirlpool while his smashed canoe was tossed in pieces down rapids, along with four hundred plant species and months and months of careful notes.

He spent several months in the Sandwich Islands, revelling in mosses and lichens and ferns and studying geographical features and semi-active volcanoes. He was perfectly happy and would have liked to have stayed longer but he knew it was time he returned to

England, so he planned to go on the next ship that came that way. Meanwhile he offered to guide a missionary round Hawaii.

"I will meet you at the village of Hilo," he said. The appointed day came, and the missionary made his way to Hilo. David Douglas was not there. The missionary waited and waited and eventually left, alone. About this time two local men heard the frightened and ferocious sounds of a trapped animal, and realised that something had fallen into a cattle trap through the rough covering of branches and earth. It was a wild bull, charging up and down in the pit and snorting with anger and fear. There too was a dead man, his body gashed by the bull, his clothes torn to ribbons. It was David Douglas. Above him, still on firm ground, sat a little black Scottish terrier guarding a bundle of dried plants and notebooks and seeds.

Nina

When Nina was five years old, her parents took her to the ballet to see a performance of *The Nutcracker*. She was a little dark-haired girl with dark eyes and a very expressive face. She sat silent and entranced, with her lips apart and her heart full of happiness. Father had told her she was going to fairyland. She had thought he had been teasing, but now she began to wonder if perhaps he had really meant it, and she waited eagerly as the stage curtains shivered a little and slowly opened.

The first scene showed a room where children and grownups were gathering for a party. There was a tall Christmas tree hung with twinkling lights and sparkling baubles and little coloured bags of sweets and beautiful dolls and exciting presents. The children danced and played and the adults handed out the gifts. Slowly the story unfolded, showing how Clara, who lived in the house, crept down again at night and watched the dolls coming to life, and how one of them turned into a handsome prince and took her to the Land of Snow.

Nina glanced at her father in the darkness. This must be what he had meant, for what could be more like fairyland than this? The whole of the stage now appeared to be a forest where every tree sparkled with frost and where snow seemed to lie thick on the ground. A fairy appeared, the Fairy of Ice and Snow, and began to dance with Clara. All around were snowflake fairies, dancing, whirling, jumping, almost floating in an unbelievable scene of shimmering beauty. Nina had never seen anything so wonderful, and in her mind she too had become a snowflake fairy, leaping, twirling, spinning through the air. In ordinary life she had great problems, and things were often bewildering and difficult, but now all her troubles were forgotten and she asked for nothing better than this.

Nina's mother was lost in thought. She was so glad to see how the little girl was enjoying the performance. There were no spoken words to confuse her. There were no explanations needed. Nina quite obviously had been transported into a different, beautiful, dreamlike world. It was unusual for Mother to be sitting in an audience. She was more often on a stage, not as a ballet dancer, but as an actress. Her family had been actors for generations, following a tradition going back three hundred years. Her husband was also an actor, and when Nina had been a baby they had often looked at her and wondered if she too would act. But they had known for two years now that this would be quite impossible. Nina was deaf. She could not hear speech or music, or children laughing, or birds singing, and because of this she had not learned to speak. Yet her world was not entirely silent, for she could catch the deep throb of very low notes of music and try to imitate a few vowel sounds that emerged from the movements of people's lips.

She had spent her babyhood touring with her parents as they acted at theatres in different parts of the country. She had often taken her afternoon nap at the back of the stage, and slept at night in many varied lodgings. When she was three her parents had moved to London, and only in the summer did the family tour again. It was essential to have a settled home for Nina so that she could go to nursery school and primary school and take lessons in speech and lip-reading. Her difficulties at school can be imagined. She heard nothing of what the teacher said. She sat in puzzled silence while the other children listened in rapt attention to stories. When they laughed, she never knew what they were laughing at.

Slowly she realised that she was different from the others. She retreated into a dream world of her own and was often bewildered and frustrated and very unhappy. Most small children are kind to those who are handicapped. They willingly lead blind children or help crippled ones, but deafness is something they do not really understand. There is nothing to see, and they are a little disconcerted by the strange sounds that deaf children utter, so it was not easy for Nina to make friends. All the same, she was a brave child, and because of her disability she had become particularly observant. She could watch and copy and slowly, slowly she could learn.

Mother and Father, of course, could usually understand her grunts and gestures and now when the ballet was over, they knew very well what she tried to tell them,

"I want to learn to dance."

They thought that in a week or two she would have forgotten about it, but she indicated perfectly plainly that she had not. She spread her arms and tripped about the room, pointing her toes and whirling round. She was showing so obviously that she wanted to learn to dance.

"I'm afraid that if she goes to dancing lessons, she will find them disappointing," said Mother to Father. "She won't hear the music or the instructions."

"She's pretty observant," replied Father. "She can watch and copy. We could let her try for a term anyway."

"Mm. I don't want her to be unhappy." Mother was doubtful about it, but she found a good dancing teacher, and Nina joined other small children once a week in a hall with a floor of smooth, creaky boards and an upright piano. Far from bringing disappointment and unhappiness, these classes opened up a new world, a new life for Nina. For a few weeks she watched the teacher and the other children carefully and followed the steps uncertainly.

Then she realised that a steady rhythm was beating its way through the floor to her feet. She could hear only a few low notes of the music. She could hear nothing of the tune and the higher chords and the trills, but she could feel the vibrations of the piano beating,

beating, telling her how fast or how slowly to move. This was wonderful. She could not express herself through speech, but she could express herself through movement, through dancing, through the feel of this exciting rhythm.

The dancing class became the highlight of her week. Here she was happy, for here she seemed to be no different from other children. Strangely enough, she seemed to be better than most. Other children sometimes took wrong steps or misjudged distances and bumped into each other, but Nina almost never did. She appeared to possess perfect rhythm and a wonderful instinctive feeling for the music she could not hear.

The dancing teacher soon realised that in this little deaf girl she had someone very special, and when Nina was seven and a half she encouraged her to take an audition at the Junior Royal Ballet School. If she passed she would be given lessons in their London class two or three times a week. Nervously one Saturday morning she joined a large group of eager little girls all hoping to be chosen for the coveted classes. Only six were selected and Nina Falaise was one of them.

.   .   .   .   .   .

Lip-reading is very difficult to learn (watch television with the sound turned off and see how little you can understand). Some people hardly move their lips at all when they speak. Some words and sounds do not show on the lips in any case, and some words can easily be mistaken for others with entirely different meanings, (ladder and letter, her and hair, racer and razor, peach and speech). Some people's mouths are half hidden by bushy beards and some people speak from behind a newspaper or a cup of tea or their own hands.

From the age of three, Nina had lip-reading lessons and lessons in speech, three or four times a week. Babies learn to talk through hearing speech around them every day. Deaf children are unable to learn this natural way. They have to learn every separate sound and every separate word. When they try to speak, they cannot hear their own voices, and they can learn only by the feel of sounds in their throats and mouths – the little pop of the lips for "p" or the breathy feeling of "h". One of Nina's teachers showed her how to pronounce consonants by using a lighted candle

and seeing whether she could make the flame flicker the right way. In spite of all the hard work, Nina was ten years old before she began to string spoken words together, and she was sixteen before she could hold a conversation using lip-reading and her own voice.

Reading too was difficult to learn, but when she was eight, words and letters seemed to fall into place and she found she was able to enjoy books and the wider world they opened out for her. Even so, school continued to be a bewildering, unhappy place, and she looked forward more than ever to the dancing lessons. There she continued to amaze her teachers. For most ballet dancers, music was the essential ingredient of their success. It told them when to start and stop. It gave them the details of speed and phrasing and rhythm. How was it possible for Nina to keep so perfectly in time, and to dance with such outstanding grace and poise? It must be something within herself – her own built-in sense of rhythm and timing. It was decided that she should try to get to White Lodge, the Royal Ballet School, for full-time training. This would mean applying for an audition at the age of ten, and Nina looked forward to it with excitement and great hope.

When eventually it took place, there seemed so many other ten-year-old girls in the room that Nina felt that she would not stand a chance. Only a few were to be selected. How could she possibly be lucky enough to be one of them? She concentrated so earnestly that it almost hurt. She did what was required of her. She spread her arms. She pointed her toes. She jumped. She stretched. She danced a few steps. She hoped and hoped that she would be chosen.

Soon it was over, and a few days later a letter came that would lift her spirits to the sky or dash all her hopes to the ground. Mother opened it and Nina stood trembling beside her, longing yet dreading to know the verdict. Anxiously she stared at Mother's lips, but really there was no need to do that, for the expression on her face told Nina the answer. She was in. She had come through the first audition with flying colours! Now there was a second audition and a medical examination to take the following March. She was healthy and strong. She had a good straight spine and long slim legs, and strong ankles and feet. If she passed the second audition there was no reason why she should not pass the medical. But there was a reason. She was deaf. The selectors realised that she would not hear the music or the instructions. She failed the medical examination and she was not given a place.

When Nina had been small she had sometimes flown into terrible temper tantrums because she could not communicate, and she felt so frustrated and full of despair. She felt like that now, but she was ten years old and she was a fighter. She was determined to become a dancer. There were other dancing schools and other ways of getting to the top. She refused to give up the struggle.

The next step was easier than she or her parents had dared to hope. She was accepted by the Rambert school of dancing, where ordinary school lessons were interspersed with training in ballet. The teachers were particularly kind and understanding, and Nina for the first time began to derive some pleasure from school work. As for the dancing, it was sheer joy, and she became interested in Indian and Spanish and modern dancing as well as in classical ballet.

One of the chief ballet instructors quickly saw that Nina had special gifts, and that her eyes did much of the work of her ears in picking up new movements and new rhythms. She thought so highly of her pupil that she soon allowed her to attend some of the adult professional classes she gave in her private studio. These

classes brought even more satisfaction to Nina than the instruction she received in the school. When she was thirteen she was given a scholarship to enable her to concentrate entirely on the adult classes and to continue her ordinary education with a private teacher.

It must have been quite difficult to fit everything into the week, as Nina always went to the morning ballet classes two hours before time in order to warm up and practise and practise and practise the steps.

. . . . . .

When Nina was sixteen her training ended. Not that a ballet dancer's training ever really ends – she continues to learn and train and practise for the whole of her dancing life. Nina had the added work of learning and practising lip-reading and speech too. Her first dancing engagement was as a cygnet in *Swan Lake*, involving a long tour of Germany. She had never been away from home before and she felt very lost and afraid. After that there were other offers.

She was a solo Spanish dancer in an open-air production of the opera *Carmen* at Macerata, Italy. She was Hermia in *Midsummer Night's Dream* in Rome. She danced in Sicily and France and she began to create her own ballets, which sometimes seemed the most rewarding experience of all. Then there was a season in Palermo, in Sicily. The ballet was *The Nutcracker* and she, Nina Falaise, was a snow fairy in a stage forest where every tree sparkled with frost and where snow seemed to lie thick on the ground. She danced and whirled and leaped and almost floated in an unbelievable scene of shimmering beauty. She remembered watching this same ballet at the age of five. She remembered longing and longing to be a snowflake fairy, and she realised now that it was that day that had been the turning point of her whole life.

She had been a little, speechless, bewildered girl at that time. Now there were dancers in the company who did not even realise yet that she was deaf, and certainly the audience would never know. They saw her only as a gifted dancer with faultless technique and perfect timing and an indescribable joy in movement.

Patchwork Pages

The Glassmakers

When people visit the Botanical Museum of Harvard University in the United States of America, they always stand amazed in one of the exhibition halls. It is full of plants and flowers, some lifesize and some enlarged. They look fresh and natural as if they have just been picked and brought indoors. There are 784 lifesize models and more than 3000 enlargements. Every one is perfect, from the threadlike stamens of a buttercup to the delicate, gossamer-thin hairs of a cactus. They look delicate and real, and only as near as half a metre can it be seen that every one, in every detail, is made of glass.

The entire collection was the work of two men, Leopold and Rudolph Blashka, a father and son, working without help from anyone else at their home near Dresden in Germany.

Generations and generations of men in the Blashka family had worked in decorative glass. They moved from Venice early in the fifteenth century to Bohemia, where they continued to develop their skills, passing down their talents from father to son, father to son, through the ages. Leopold and Rudolph were both born in Bohemia, but moved later to Germany, where Leopold, the father, made beautiful glass models of sea-creatures – jellyfish, sea snails and sea anemones – which he sold to museums all over the world. He was a devoted naturalist, and he had many books on marine biology as well as books on the flowers of Europe and America. He also kept sea-aquaria in his house, so that he could observe live creatures at first hand. Rudolph, his son, was also a devoted naturalist and had more opportunity of travel and study than his father, so the two men worked together, with no other assistant.

At that time in America plans were made for a new botanical museum, and when consideration was given to possible exhibits, it was decided that something more interesting and attractive was needed than just pictures and pressed flowers or dried plants. Professor

Goodale, who was in charge, searched at home and abroad for some satisfactory way of displaying an ordered arrangement of three-dimensional plants. He examined and discarded models of wax and models of papier-maché. Then in the zoology museum next door he saw a few glass models of jellyfish and sea-anemones. They were of great beauty and delicacy, and finding that the makers were Leopold and Rudolph Blashka, he travelled at once to Germany to meet them in their studio near Dresden. There he asked Leopold if he would make models for the museum, but Leopold at first refused.

"We have plenty of work with marine animals," he said. "Besides I do not think we could make satisfactory models of flowers."

This surprised Professor Goodale, for on a shelf in the very room were a few orchids made of glass, looking as if they had just been brought in from a greenhouse.

"But those orchids," he protested. "They are just the kind of thing we need. When did you make those?"

"Oh a long time ago," replied Leopold. "Nearly twenty years ago. I made about sixty models of orchids for a museum in Belgium, but the whole collection was destroyed in a fire in 1868."

Eventually Professor Goodale persuaded the Blashkas to make a few samples for him, and later

they consented to work for him on a half-time basis. Finally they gave up the marine models, and worked entirely on flowers and plants. They never employed any assistants and they worked together until 1895 when Leopold died. Rudolph then continued alone until his own death in 1936 – at the age of 86.

The work is of exquisite craftsmanship. Each leaf, each petal is made of clear glass, pulled out and shaped with simple instruments in intensely hot flame, with home-made natural colours applied and burned into them. Every vein, every tiny dot, is carefully included, and a simple wrong movement by these two patient, devoted men could have ruined hours of work.

Sadly, neither of the Blashkas ever saw their entire collection in place, but it is still examined yearly by as many as two hundred thousand admiring visitors.

Spoonerisms

The Reverend William Archibald Spooner lived from 1844 to 1930. He was a brilliant scholar and he lectured on ancient history and philosophy at Oxford, and eventually became warden of New College. He did valuable work for the college and also for various charities in the district. His name is universally known, and he became a legend in his own lifetime. Ironically, his fame rests, not on his reputation as a great scholar or a fine warden, but on a strange absent-minded lapse of speech. He would mix the first letters, or sometimes the first syllables of words. For example, it is said that he once announced the hymn "Loving Shepherd of Thy Sheep" as "Shoving Leopard of Thy Sheep" and another hymn "Conquering Kings their Titles Take" as "Kinquering Congs their Titles Take".

These speech errors are now known as "spoonerisms". So many spoonerisms were attributed to him that they are probably not all genuine. They are, after all, easy to invent. We hear, no doubt falsely, of someone "fighting a liar on the lawn" and of someone else having "a half-warmed fish within him" (a half-formed wish). Imagine the feelings of a lazy student when he was told that he had "tasted two worms" and could leave Oxford by the "town drain".

Not only, apparently, did the Reverend Spooner

mix up initial sounds, but he sometimes transposed whole words, as on the occasion when he asked a waitress for "a glass bun and a bath of milk". Even more surprising, he preached a whole sermon one Sunday on Aristotle. Then as he was leaving the pulpit, he paused and apologised to the congregation, saying,

"I'm sorry, but when I said Aristotle, I really meant St Paul."

There were many stories too of his general absent-mindedness. He once asked someone to lunch so that he might meet a man called Casson.

"But I am Casson," was the reply.

"Never mind," said Spooner. "Come all the same."

Then there was the incident of seeing an old lady friend off on a train. He handed her a tip, and gave a farewell kiss to the porter.

A Strange Custom

Outside the churchyard gate in the village of Shebbear in Devon there stands a very old oak tree. Under its shade is a large stone, quite unlike any other stone in the district. Scientists say it must have been left there when the ice melted at the end of the Ice Age, but local people have grown up with the idea that it was dropped by the devil, and that it must be turned once a year in order to prevent him causing any trouble in the village.

No one knows when the custom started, but the stone is turned faithfully every year on the evening of November the fifth, though it has no connection with the Guy Fawkes celebrations of that date. The stone is very heavy and it is the church bell-ringers who turn it, using crowbars. Before and after the turning they give a noisy, jangling discordant performance on the bells. This is to frighten the devil away from the district.

In 1940 it was decided to drop the custom. The nation was at war and a blackout was in force, and the night of November the fifth was not marked in any special way even for Guy Fawkes. Many people however felt that now more than ever it might be wise to keep the devil in check, so a week later the stone was duly turned in the darkness, and has been turned once a year ever since.

Mother Seacole

Her name was Mary Seacole and she was born in Jamaica of a Jamaican mother and a Scottish father. She had black frizzy hair and a brown skin and she was a most unusual person, full of courage and compassion. She grew up at a time when British redcoat soldiers were stationed at Kingston, Jamaica, and she helped her mother to run a boarding-house and café for them. They appreciated her cheerful friendliness, and often confided in her, telling her about their homes and families and their problems. She understood their ways and their humour and she knew just what they liked to eat. She was interested too, in medicine and nursing, and thought that perhaps one day she might go and work somewhere among the sick.

Seacole was her married name, but her husband died early and she was left with a nice sum of money from him and also from her parents. What should she do with it? She decided to see something of the world. She travelled for several years, learning more about medicine wherever she went. She visited California and Panama among other places, and in the autumn of 1854 she reached London. There, the conversation was all about the war taking place in the Crimea on the shores of the Black Sea. There was talk of bravery and tragedy and hardship and there was talk of Florence Nightingale, a woman of rich and gentle upbringing, who had gone to the battleground with thirty-eight nurses to care for the sick and wounded soldiers.

Mary Seacole listened to harrowing descriptions of the terrible state of the military hospitals. She heard of the shabby, inadequate buildings, of the cold and the filth, and the almost complete lack of medical necessities, or even of the necessities for ordinary decent living.

As the winter advanced there were heartening stories of Florence Nightingale's work. She was in charge of five thousand men. She was working wonders it was said, bringing order and cleanliness and healing out of what had seemed impossible chaos. She was working day and night, and in the darkness she always walked along eight kilometres of beds, holding a lamp and bringing comfort and hope to the sick and wounded. The men adored her. They almost worshipped her, it was said.

Mary Seacole made up her mind at once. This was the sort of work for her. She would go out to the Crimea and become one of Florence Nightingale's nurses. It was not so easy. She called at the war office in London and offered her services. As so often happens when permission is sought for anything, she was sent from

one department to another. No one seemed to have the necessary authority to accept her.

"No more nurses are being added to the list," she was told at last. She was bitterly disappointed, but undaunted.

"All right. If I can't go officially, I'll go unofficially," she thought. "If I can't be a nurse, I'll open a cafe in the war zone instead – like the one we had at home in Jamaica."

She had always loved the British redcoats and had looked upon them as her sons. They had often regarded her as a sort of universal mother, and had christened her affectionately "Mother Seacole".

In January she set sail for Constantinople, going ashore en route at Gibraltar and Malta. Walking through the streets in both these places, she was hailed by army officers who had known her in Kingston.

"Dear old Mother Seacole!" they cried. She told them of her plans.

"Oh fine!" they agreed. "The men will be delighted to see you."

The voyage continued to Constantinople. Then there was a trip across the Black Sea to Balaclava, where Mary Seacole intended to open her boarding-house café. But first it had to be built. There was plenty of driftwood and wreckage floating in the harbour, and she engaged some Turkish labourers and two sailors to haul it ashore and to erect a building with storehouses, sheds and dormitories, and most important, a kitchen and a long dining room. It was named the "British Hotel" and it was topped by a flagpole and a Union Jack.

By early summer it was finished, and equipped liberally with stores from Constantinople. There seemed no shortage of food, and Mary Seacole was an excellent cook. She provided roast beef, mutton, fowl, cold ham and tongue, lobsters, oysters, salmon, hot soups, delicious puddings and cakes and jam tarts. It was not surprising that the British Hotel rapidly became the most popular place in the Crimea. Good Mrs Seacole started work every morning before dawn, brewing coffee for her "sons" coming in from night duty. Then for the rest of the day there would be redcoats, young and old, crowding into the dining room, calling a checry word into her kitchen, settling down to a tasty snack or a good meal in the warmth and welcome, away from the trenches and the mud and the blood of the battlefield. Not only did Mrs Seacole supply food, but she was soon making herbal medicines as well, and many men considered them better than the physic provided by their own medical officers.

"Mother Seacole's medicines will cure anything," they declared. Her talents lay in other directions too. When entertainments were organised by the men, it was Mrs Seacole who would become wardrobe mistress. She would lend her own large, bright dresses to the entertainers. She would alter jackets and trim caps and make artificial curls.

As the months went by and Christmas approached and the weather became steadily more icy, there was considerable anxiety about her.

"She comes from a hot country," said some. "It's possible that she will not live through the winter." But dear Mother Seacole battled on bravely. She turned out Christmas puddings by the score and hundreds of mince pies.

Mother Seacole's charges in the café were reasonable and she gave good value for money. She also gave a great deal free out of the goodness of her heart. Mule trains often passed her door, taking wounded and sick soldiers down to the harbour to await hospital ships. Sometimes as many as two hundred men were kept waiting for hours in temperatures well below freezing point. Mother Seacole would take kettles and mugs and make hot tea for them. She would gently adjust bandages and speak words of cheer and comfort.

Even in the heat of battle her sturdy figure could be seen, going from one man to another. She carried a large bag containing medicine and bandages and nourishing dainties. When men were wounded she usually reached them before the stretcher bearers. Heedless of her own safety she often had narrow escapes.

"Down, mother, down!" men would cry as shots whirled over her. The wounded needed help and

comfort, and if sometimes one or two of the enemy lay helpless among her sons, then they too would benefit from her kindness.

The war ended. Relieved, excited, the redcoats prepared to return home. There were many small gifts and farewell notes left in the café for Mother Seacole. Then as columns of soldiers marched past on their way to the harbour, there were cheers and waves to her as she stood at the door, and numerous men stepped out of line a moment to grasp her hand in gratitude.

Then she had the mournful task of clearing up the British Hotel. She had bills to pay, and stock to clear, and she was nearly bankrupt. Worse than this, there was silence in the building. There was no one stamping in out of the cold for a cup of coffee and a chat. There was no one to grasp her affectionately round the waist with the cry of "dear old Mother Seacole". Many of those bright young men lay buried around Balaclava and Inkerman. The rest had marched away. Her sons had gone.

Mary Seacole went back to Jamaica. No doubt she was glad to feel the warmth of the sun, but her heart was sad because her work was done.

Most of the information for this story comes from the book *Colonel's Lady and Camp-follower* by Piers Compton, published by Robert Hale Ltd

The Unsinkable Ship

On April the tenth 1912 the White Star liner, *Titanic*, left Southampton for New York. She was the largest ship afloat, and also the most luxurious. Her measurements were such that if she were stood on end (as an advertisement depicted) she would have been taller than Cologne Cathedral in Germany, taller than the Pyramid of Gizah in Egypt, and taller even than the Woolworth Building in New York. She was so big that when she had been launched from the Belfast shipyard the year before, twenty-three tonnes of grease had been needed to slide her down the slipway, a journey that had taken her just sixty-two seconds. Her anchor had been dragged to the ship by a team of twenty horses, and it was fixed in place with enormous, thick chains – each link weighing more than a well-built man. Her decks rose one above the other like a building eleven storeys high, with four great funnels on the top, on a base of sixteen watertight compartments. She was so well planned, it was said, that she was unsinkable. A ship like a floating town, and she was unsinkable!

Outside, she was an impressive sight. Inside, she was the last word in luxury. There were grand staircases and dining rooms, cafés, reading and writing rooms and smoking rooms. There were richly-panelled walls and soft, deep carpets. There were heavy, leather armchairs and scintillating chandeliers. There were well-fitted cabins for ordinary people, and wonderful staterooms for the very rich, with table lamps and electric heaters, and with adjoining accommodation for their servants and their children's nurses. There were turkish baths and swimming baths, shops and a gymnasium. There was a band to provide dance music and entertainment. It was said there was even a herd of cows to provide fresh milk.

When the ship left Southampton there were about 2224 people on board (afterwards there was a little doubt about exactly *how* many). There were men, women, children, babies. There were rich and not so rich – first class, second class, third class. Some men had saved a long time in order to pay the fare for themselves or their families to emigrate to America. Some were going on business, or to visit relatives. Some of the rich were going just for the pleasure of the trip or simply because they were eager to be present on the maiden voyage of this wonderful ship. Some people had only the fewest of possessions, packed in a single small bag. Others had as many as fourteen trunks, filled with perhaps seventy frocks and as many pairs of gloves. Most people were happy, excited and contented with their lot, whatever it might be.

So the *Titanic* sailed. The passengers chatted and laughed, the band played, and days passed in idle pleasure. Meanwhile the engineers, the stewards, the kitchen staff and all the other members of the crew from Captain Smith downwards were working hard to ensure that everything went smoothly – as smoothly as the sea itself seemed to flow on the first few days of the voyage.

Then came April the fourteenth. The night was cold, clear and bright. The *Titanic* sped calmly along in its own pool of light, created by hundreds of winking portholes and the well-lit windows of the public rooms. The sea ahead was dark and smooth, and the sky was filled with stars. The engines chugged over in a steady rhythm, a comforting sound for the people who had gone early to bed. Some were already asleep. Others were still standing about, enjoying the beauty of the night or chatting from the deep armchairs in the smoking room of this beautiful, happy, unsinkable ship. Time ticked on – ten o'clock, eleven, half past eleven, twenty to twelve. Twenty to twelve. Eleven-forty. It was a fateful moment. Greenish, bluish, gleaming in the lights, a gigantic iceberg stood suddenly in the path of the ship, towering above the upper decks, scraping cruelly along the side, tearing a hundred-metre gash in the lower decks, and opening the way in one of the boiler rooms for the surge of the sea.

Many people slept on without even being aware of the thud, the rumbling, the quivering of the ship. Some were awakened by the jolt, and one or two were amazed to see a wall of gleaming ice outside their portholes. One man, whose porthole was open, saw broken lumps of ice tumble into his cabin.

Some of the people in the smoking room ran out on deck and caught a glimpse of the gigantic iceberg before it slid silently away into the darkness, but most people had no idea what had happened. Even when the words, "We've hit an iceberg" buzzed round the ship, they were followed by the assurance, "There's no danger though".

Some people who had come out of their cabins to investigate were lulled into false security and went back to bed again. Some of the third-class passengers on the lower decks, however, found water swirling round their cabin floors, and realised at once that something had gone wrong somewhere.

Captain Smith at this time was on the bridge. He was a much loved and respected man, and this was, in every sense of the word, his last voyage. He would have retired some months before, but he had agreed to take the *Titanic* on its maiden trip. He could not possibly have imagined that the ship might founder, or be overtaken by any disaster, but now there was water pouring into the mail room and creeping on to the squash court. By five past midnight the captain had given his numerous orders, starting with two of the most vital – all passengers on decks and all lifeboats uncovered. At once the stewards made the rounds of their cabins, banging on the doors, flinging them open saying, "On deck at once, wearing lifebelts!"

It was interesting to note what different passengers wore in the way of clothing and what they tried to take with them. As the groups of chattering, questioning people collected on board their own decks there were some in nothing but night attire, some in fur coats or evening wraps, some with blankets round their shoulders, some in all sorts of warm underclothing and overgarments, some immaculately dressed in their best clothes or country tweeds, and one and all wearing, or struggling to put on, a lifebelt, which never for a moment had they thought they would be using. These were the days when well-dressed ladies and gentlemen wore hats, so there were even a great many unsuitable objects of headgear in evidence, while footgear ranged from high-heeled evening shoes to bedroom slippers or boots. Some people had stuffed their pockets with money or important papers. Some carried jewel boxes or a framed photograph or a book, or a snack of some sort. There were even two or three pet dogs.

At this time radio was in its infancy, but at twelve-fifteen the *Titanic* began sending out signals for help. Meanwhile the crew were uncoiling the ropes of the lifeboats which swung from their davits twenty metres above the sea. Even including four collapsible canvas boats, there was accommodation in the lifeboats for no more than 1178 people. The *Titanic* had 2224 aboard. In any case she was unsinkable so there was no need to worry. Women and children, climbing gingerly and unwillingly into the boats, expected to be back on board in an hour or so, when the *Titanic*'s trouble had been remedied.

Fortunately the sea was still calm and smooth, though the night was bitterly cold. The eight bandsmen assembled on deck and played loud and cheerful music. On the different decks, various arguments broke out at the lifeboats. A few women refused to go into them without their husbands. A few refused to go at all. A few men tried to break the sea rule of "women and children first".

Strangely enough with all this commotion, the crew member at the very stern of the ship was still keeping his silent watch, quite unaware of what was going on. Suddenly he saw a lifeboat floating in the water. In amazement he phoned the bridge.

"Do you know there's a lifeboat afloat?"

"Who are you?" he was asked.

"The watch at the stern."

"Good gracious! Don't you know we hit an iceberg? Come on to the bridge at once and bring some rockets with you."

The decks were beginning to slope rather badly now, and some passengers who foolishly took the risk of returning to their cabins for belongings found water swirling round their feet or surging over the stairs. The *Titanic* might be unsinkable but she seemed to be getting rather wet.

One by one the lifeboats creaked and clattered from

their davits and were rowed away a little distance to wait for orders. Two crew members were supposed to go in each one, but it did not always work out that way. In fact there was a great deal of confusion. Many people showed great bravery and presence of mind but others tried to rush out of turn on to the boats. Most of the lifeboats were built to carry sixty-five people, yet some of them pulled away with only twenty-eight, or even fewer aboard; while on the ever more sloping decks of the *Titanic*, groups of people swarmed to get on to boats and found that they had already left.

In the boats now, several titled ladies were rowing vigorously, children were shivering with cold and everyone was staring at the great ship, its four masts rising in the clear night sky, its rows and rows of

portholes still ablaze with lights, its bandsmen still playing gallantly without a thought for their own safety.

In the engine room too, every man was still at his post, trying to keep the heart of the ship beating, trying to fight against the encroaching sea. Now even more terrible moments came as the ship tipped like a child's toy, with its bows and bridge beneath the waves and its stern standing out of the water, crowded with the people who had been fast and nimble enough to get to it. Knowing that everyone must sooner or later slide down into the sea, many people preferred to forestall the danger by jumping into the icy waters and swimming for their lives. A thoughtful crew member threw out deck chairs and dining room chairs for survivors to cling to. Those who did not jump waited with astounding outward calm – saying goodbyes and giving messages to each other to pass on if they should be saved. The captain walked among his crew saying,

"Save yourselves boys. You've done all you can. Each man for himself now."

The water now was awash with ropes and chairs and planks, with clothes and boxes and potted palms and with every conceivable object. People, rich and poor, slid and tumbled down into the sea. Bandsmen and their instruments joined the human landslide. The

funnels fell. The lights went out. The great ship stood
for a few moments upright on her bows, taller, as the
advertisements had said, than Cologne Cathedral, taller
than the Pyramid of Gizah, taller than the Woolworth
Building in New York. From the lifeboats, many
people watched as the great ship then slid down into
the water and the sea closed over her for ever. Many
watched, but many others could not bear to see her
die – the great and beautiful *Titanic*, the ship that could
never sink!

It was now twenty past two at night. Hundreds of
heads bobbed about in the ice-cold water, as swimmers
and non-swimmers struggled for their lives. Hundreds
of voices called out for help. From the comparative

safety of the lifeboats some people urged the rowers to go back and try to rescue the drowning, but others in the same boats urged them not to risk the lives of those already aboard. There were many acts of bravery that night, but there were also many acts of selfishness and cowardice.

Of the ships that picked up the *Titanic*'s radio calls for help, it was the Cunard liner *Carpathia* that effected a rescue. She was a small ship, only a quarter of the *Titanic*'s tonnage. Her normal speed was fourteen knots but she did seventeen in her race to give help that night. At four o'clock in the morning she reached the position that had been described in the wireless call, but there was no sign of the *Titanic*. Captain Rostron of the *Carpathia* peered out in disbelief. There was no *Titanic*, but there were many lifeboats drifting on a sea now growing less calm. In the greyness of the approaching dawn they could be seen scattered over a wide area, and with them there were numerous icebergs – small ones and giant ones that had broken away from a not so distant, incredible expanse of ice. Recalling the scene later, Captain Rostron felt that he must have received divine guidance as he steered his ship that night.

At ten past four the first lifeboat was rescued. Some of the survivors were hoisted up the side of the

Carpathia, but those who were sufficiently agile climbed up a rope ladder and were helped, stumbling and cold and thankful, into the rescue ship. One by one the lifeboats were picked up. Some of the people were too numb and miserable to notice any details, but others remembered always the gleam of the dazzling icebergs, the brilliance of the morning star and the beauty of the small crescent moon.

Then there were warm blankets and hot drinks, and frantic enquiries for lost relatives and friends; and two or three hours later a service was held in the *Carpathia*'s lounge, and passengers from the two ships gave united thanks for those who had been saved. It was ten to nine when Captain Rostron, certain that there could be no more survivors, gave the signal for his ship to steam ahead for New York.

.   .   .   .   .   .

To this day there is some doubt about the exact number of people who perished in the *Titanic*, but it was round about fifteen hundred. None of the engineers was saved and none of the pursers, none of the ship's boys or the postal clerks, none of the bandsmen. Of the eighty-four men of the stokehold watch only eight survived. So the list goes on and then it is remembered that for 2224 people on the ship there was lifeboat accommodation for little more than half of them. More time and thought and care had been given to the interior decoration of the public rooms than to the possible need to save lives. In any case the regulations about the number of lifeboats to be carried had been drawn up in 1894 when no ship was bigger than a quarter of the *Titanic*'s size.

After the disaster of course this rule was changed. The winter shipping lane was also altered and brought further south, and an international Ice Patrol was established to keep icebergs out of the path of ships. Radio rules were also tightened. It was an example of locking the stable door after the horse had bolted, but at least it made shipping safer in the years that followed.

.   .   .   .   .   .

And there lies the *Titanic* deep down at the bottom of the sea. The impact must have twisted and smashed and crumbled her frame. The pressure of the water must have reduced her, at least in part, to an unrecognisable mass of rubble. Yet over the years there have been many plans to locate her, to photograph her, even to raise her, plans which so far have come to nothing. Only the future will tell if any of them are likely to succeed.

Christopher

This is a true story. It is sad and happy and full of courage and promise and hope. It is about Christopher, whose life seemed "spoiled at its beginning". He could not walk or use his hands. He could not sit up without support. He could not hold up his head for more than a few minutes at a time. He could not wash himself or feed himself, and even swallowing was very difficult. He could not use his muscles, and sometimes he was overwhelmed by strong, jerky spasms of movement that he could not control. All this was bad enough, but worst of all was the fact that he could not speak. There were all sorts of things he wanted to say – all sorts of things he wanted to write, for he had a bright and lively mind, imprisoned in a helpless body.

He bravely and cheerfully accepted most of his terrible handicaps, but he longed and longed to talk. Even so he had a system of communication with his family which he had used since babyhood. It was a sort of code of facial expressions and eye-to-eye contact. Sometimes it would turn into a kind of guessing game with his mother. When he had given her the vital clue, she would say,

"Is it this or this?" Then he would stare at the right thing. This of course was often a very slow method. He understood all that was said to him. He could answer "yes" by raising his eyes, or "no" by glancing sideways. He could even joke with his sister Yvonne and communicate with his friend Alex, who often spent the weekend with him.

He could not play with toys or games. He could not read unless someone held a book for him and turned the pages. No one knew how much he really could read or how much of it he could understand. There was only one sort of game he could play. Sitting by himself in his wheelchair, he could only play with words, silently sorting them into delicious patterns in his mind, putting them together to make poems or stories or just thoughts. He used long, complicated words and melodious phrases for a boy of his age, like,

"anonymous opportunities", or

"lonely, lost, loose", or

"among life's indigent agnostics", or

"friendly fulsome fears of frolicking flashes of foibles".

No one could tell that he knew such words, and no one knew that he amused himself in this way. He longed and longed to write or record his poems and stories, but they had to remain locked in his mind.

Every day his mother took him to a special school for handicapped children in Dublin. Some of the children could read aloud, and some could use their hands or walk on crutches, but Christopher could only listen and watch. The teachers and physiotherapists were kind and patient. They felt sure that Christopher was a bright boy, and they tried every possible way of helping him. They tried to teach him to type. If he could learn to type he would be able to type his thoughts and "speak" to people through the typewriter. Could he gather just enough strength to enable him to press the keys? They tried his right hand and his left hand but it was no good. They tried his right foot and his left foot without success. They thought of his mouth and they tried a method of suck and blow that some paralysed and spastic people were able to use, but this too, was unsuccessful. "What about a chin stick?" someone suggested, but this also failed.

"What about a head stick?" A teacher strapped a stick to Christopher's head. It was called a unicorn. He could move his head a tiny, tiny bit, but not enough to enable him to get the unicorn to touch the right letter. He tried and tried. Sometimes he would almost, almost touch a letter he wanted, and then he would be gripped by a spasm that would jerk the unicorn away. His failure was total and all his hopes were dashed. His mother was given an electric typewriter for him to practise on at home, but after a while she found his frantic, desperate efforts so distressing that she gave up trying and put the typewriter away.

Christopher was awake a long time that night, begging and praying for some form of communication with which to express what he called his "alert, myriad, brilliant, milling mind".

When he was eleven years old, a new drug came into use to help spastic children. It was supposed to help them to relax a little and to keep the spasms within bounds. Christopher's doctor tried it on him – a very small dose at first, increasing in size as the days passed. His mother noticed that it did help just a little to relax the jerks and spasms.

"Try typing again at home," suggested one of his teachers hopefully. "You might find it a bit easier now." Christopher did not raise his eyes for "yes" and he did not like to glance sideways for "no". He remembered his frantic, frantic efforts before, and he simply could not, would not try again.

Next week the teacher said,

"Did you try the typewriter again, Christopher?" Christopher could not raise his eyes to say "yes" and he was ashamed to look sideways to say "no" but the teacher could tell by his face that he had not tried.

That weekend his mother put the typewriter on the table in front of his wheelchair, and fastened the unicorn stick to his head.

"Try, Christy," she begged. "The relaxing drug may make it easier for you." She sat beside him and cupped her hand gently round his chin. Christopher tried bravely to push the thought of failure from his mind, and he made a stab at the machine with his stick. It touched "p" very softly, but just enough to make the letter visible on the paper. He touched another letter – "o". He typed a whole word, a strange, unusual word for a child to use, "polarised". He was writing a poem – a four-line poem from his own mind, a poem about his handicap with strange, long words.

Slowly, slowly he tapped out the letters, his mother holding his chin and watching in wonder and amazement. The four short lines took a long, long time and when they were finished, Christopher's face was full

of triumph and joy. His mother's eyes were wet with tears. It was as if eleven years of darkness had been pierced at last by a shaft of light. Lovingly, gratefully, she stroked her son's hair and said,

"Christy, is that the sort of mind you have?"

"Yes," he replied with his eyes. "Yes, yes, yes."

Now life became very different for Christopher. The loving partnership between his mother and himself enabled him to express all his emotions. He typed many of the strange, wonderful word patterns that had been going round in his head all this time – the unspoken longings and feelings and imaginings. With her hand supporting his chin, he poured his imprisoned thoughts into typing.

"Poured" is not quite the right word to use. Typing was a slow, slow process, every word taking about fifteen minutes to write. Sometimes he could not direct the unicorn to the letter he wanted at all. Sometimes he could not put enough pressure behind it or a spasm would jerk it away again and again. On a bad day he could write no more than five words in as many hours. On a good day he might write thirty, and once after working all day till half past nine at night, he typed two hundred and sixty words, by which time both he and his mother were completely exhausted.

His father, his sister, his doctors and teachers and physiotherapists were delighted. They had always thought that Christopher was a bright boy. They had always thought that he had a good brain locked up in this impossible, tangled, jerky, helpless body. All these years they had been searching for a key to unlock the door and set his intelligence free. Now they had found it.

They had not known before that Christopher could even spell or put sentences together. Now in this slow, labouring manner he was writing stories and poems, showing a vivid imagination and a most unusual way with words. His words were so difficult and strange and uncommon that many of them were seldom used even by adults. Where had he learned them all? How had his mind become so crowded, so alive with such descriptive, fascinating thoughts?

"He sometimes listens to programmes like 'Mastermind' on television," his father told people, "but I've never heard some of Christy's words on television."

Where *did* Christopher get his words from? How had he built up such a large, unusual vocabulary? His own answer, given slowly and joyfully on his typewriter was that as he typed his thoughts, "brilliant, bright, boiling words poured into his mind, sometimes with such ferocity, that he felt spoiling confusion creep across his turbulent, creative mind".

One day his Uncle John wrote to Christopher's mother enclosing a newspaper cutting about a "Literary Contest for the Handicapped". Mother read the particulars aloud to Christopher and seeing the interest on his face she asked,

"Shall we go in for it?"

"Yes, yes," Christopher's eyes rolled upwards.

"What will you write about?"

Christopher thought for some time, and eventually decided to write an essay about his own life and about his mother's brave, never-ending struggle to look after him and to make his terrible handicaps as bearable as possible.

He called his essay "A Mammy Encomium". "Encomium" means "a formal high-flown expression of praise". It is a word used very rarely, and perhaps only Christopher would have thought of using it.

In it he told how he was handicapped from birth so that "life was spoiled at its beginning" – "a lonely, lost life". He showed a sense of humour, great courage, and a faith in God. He put his word patterns together in such a way that sometimes the meaning behind them was difficult to understand, though out of the tangled sentences there often shone something that looked like brilliance.

It was a long essay and it took hours and hours of typing, a patient struggle for Christopher with his unicorn stick, and his mother with her hand under his chin. At last it was finished,

A Mammy Encomium
by Christopher Nolan of Dublin in Eire.

Father put it in a long envelope and posted it and it went on its way to London in company with the family's hopes and dreams.

There was a long wait. Then one day a phone call came. Christopher's essay was so different, so unusual that it could not really be compared with those of other children. He had been awarded a special prize, and he and his mother were offered a flight to London to receive it. This was exciting enough, but it led to something even more exciting a few months later.

Meanwhile Christopher had grown too old for his clinic school, and though it kept him for an extra year he had to leave when he was twelve. Where was he to go? What school would accept a boy with such enormous handicaps? What school would accept a boy who could take no active part in any of the lessons, who could not answer questions or even ask them, who could not write or do tests or look after himself? If no school would take him, Christopher would just have to sit at home in his wheelchair.

The staff of a large comprehensive school decided to save him from this. They expected all sorts of difficulties, but really there were none. The boys and girls in Christopher's class gladly gave him their help and their friendship. They pushed his wheelchair

from one room to another. They included him in their conversations and their jokes. The boys even delighted him sometimes by taking him on the football field and pushing him back and forth in the way of the ball so that when it zoomed on to his foot, he could really feel part of the game and the excitement. He quickly became an important and valuable member of the school.

At first the teachers did not find it quite so easy to accept him as the children did. They found it disconcerting to address someone who could not speak. It was like talking into the air. Was he listening? How much could he understand? Was he really getting any benefit from the lessons? Certainly he was! He was learning English, Irish, mathematics, history, geography, and in his second year he added German, French and science. He also listened to the singing lessons and watched art and physical education. His mother came at lunch time, bringing him a flask of tea, and that was all he needed. He was very happy indeed to share in the lives of ordinary children in an ordinary school.

And what was the exciting event that resulted from his prize-winning essay? A Sunday paper reported the news and told his story and published a happy picture of him sprawling in the grass. It also printed some of his strange and beautiful poems, and shortly afterwards it opened a fund to buy a special "Pet" micro-computer for him that would make his typing easier to do. The machine would cost £2000, and within a few weeks people had sent donations towards it, amounting to £25000. The gifts came from all over the world – Western Europe, Malaysia, Canada, both Americas, Australia, North Africa. There were small gifts from old people and spastic children and large gifts from schools and firms. The Handicapped Children's Aid Committee agreed to buy the machine outright, and the firm that manufactured the "Pet" offered to supply machines at half price to Christopher and ten other people as well.

Students and experts in computers and electronics offered help and programmes and advice. Adaptations had to be made to the "Pet" to make it suit Christopher's particular problems, and one of the experts spent a week or more with him in Ireland seeing what was needed and then having the machine changed accordingly. At first, when the micro-computer was set up in Christopher's home, he was too excited to get any results from it. He was shaken with jerky spasms, but as the days went by and the doctor's relaxing drug took effect, it seemed as if a whole new world were about to open up before him.

Sitting in his wheelchair, Christopher faced a screen

on which were shown the letters of the alphabet as well as some common combinations like *ing*, *ist*, *qui*, *wh* and some small words such as *the*, *I*, *his*, *and*, *but*. There were also punctuation marks and the instruction "rub out". A tiny patch of light moved from letter to letter, symbol to symbol, and when it reached the one Christopher wanted, he was to touch a switch with his chin and that letter or symbol would be recorded in the computer's memory and shown on the screen. In this way, words and sentences would be built up and then typed on paper automatically.

The computer experts had also produced programmes to enable him to play board games, and they made adaptations to the machine so that he could control the light, put his radio on and off or ring a bell to call someone. He and his family were filled with excitement and happiness. The prospects appeared to be wonderful, wonderful! Now at last the unicorn could be put aside. But could it?

For many weeks Christopher remained hopeful, but try as he would, he could never anticipate the exact moment to touch the chin switch. The efforts made him so tense that his spasms became worse and the faithful unicorn had to be brought back into service. Disappointed as he must have been, Christopher faced the problems bravely, as always.

Further adaptations were made to the computer, and Christopher used it now as a typewriter, pressing the keys with the unicorn. Even so, this was much easier to do than it had been on the old typewriter. The tiniest touch would print the symbol or correct an error, or store his poems and stories away in the computer's memory; and technological research was continuing all the time. One day, perhaps, Christopher might yet be able to use the movements of his eyes to work the typewriter.

Meanwhile money still poured into the "Christopher Nolan Fund" until there was more than £40 000. Christopher was delighted. He wanted it all to be used to help other people who had a communication problem like his own. So the computer experts set to work adapting machines for other children. Every handicapped, speechless person is different. Perhaps one can just point with his foot. Another may have a tiny movement in her thumb. For most of them, there is now some hope of better things.

When Christopher was eleven and was first typing with the unicorn, he wrote about his "lonely, lost life" that was "spoiled at its beginning". Now his patience and courage is providing real help for many, many other people. His own imprisoned intelligence has been set free. He writes many poems and stories, and expresses his thoughts and emotions. He lives a far fuller life than he can ever have expected. And because of him, many other people too will find release.

.   .   .   .   .   .

Since the above was written, Christopher has had a book published. It consists of a collection of his stories and poems and is called *Dam-Burst of Dreams. The Writings of Christopher Nolan*. The publishers are Weidenfeld and Nicolson, and Christopher is sharing the royalties with the Christopher Nolan Trust.

Woman in the Wilderness

Summer had ended in Alaska. A few men were still employed in remote logging camps. A number of lonely prospectors were still searching for gold-bearing rock. Don Martin and his partner, Sam, had separated for the winter. They had found a profitable mine a few years before, and they worked in it every summer. They tunnelled into the canyon, hacking away at the rock, which was liberally sprinkled with specks of yellow gold.

Sam had left on Friday, but Don and his wife Martha had stopped a few days longer to clear up before they went home. They had a comfortable town house thirty-one hours' boat journey up the coast but they usually spent the summer together in a lone cabin near the mine in company with their twelve-year-old son, Lloyd. Lloyd had gone now because school had started, and he was spending a few nights with friends, the Smiths, until his parents returned.

Don and Martha had to collect more wood for future fires. They had to put things away, pack a few bags and close the cabin up for the winter. But first they wanted to take their mail to the mailboat which would be calling across the bay.

"I'll go tomorrow," said Don. "Coming with me?"

Martha hesitated a moment between yes and no, then she said,

"I think I'll stay here and finish clearing up. I'll come down to the beach cabin to see you off though."

The beach cabin was new. It was at the bottom of the hill, almost at the edge of the sea and convenient for the boats, the Martins' only means of transport. They had a small cabin cruiser and a little rowing boat and another small boat with an outboard motor. In the morning, very early, Don took the last of these. He filled the petrol tank and started the motor.

"Take care of yourself," he said, "I'll soon be back." He waved his hand, sailed round a small island and was gone.

Martha did not go back up the hill at once. She spent two or three hours cleaning and tidying the cabin cruiser. Then she put the beach cabin in order, slung Don's gun across her shoulders and started to climb. The gun was a safety measure, because bears used the same trail from the upper cabin to the lower. In fact bears had made and used the trail long, long before men and women had ever gone to Alaska.

Halfway up the hill the wind began to blow. Trees swayed wildly and rain came down in a sudden deluge. In a few moments Martha was soaked through, but at last she reached the cabin and soon she was safely inside. She lit a fire and took all her wet clothes off, and wondered and worried about Don. He would have met the mailboat and be on his way back by now. Wind and rain beat on the cabin, and it creaked and shook alarmingly. She prayed that Don would be kept safe. She put her hands protectively over her abdomen, for she was carrying a baby. It was due to be born in three months' time. She would have to start making some clothes for it as soon as she was back in town and able to buy material.

. . . . . .

Late in the afternoon the rain stopped and the wind died down. Don would soon be back now. No doubt he had found somewhere to shelter among the many islands during the storm. Meanwhile, Martha decided to walk to the mine and make sure no tools had been left lying around outside. She slung the gun across her shoulder. The air was clean and fresh, but a lot of mud had been washed down in places, and there were many broken branches littering the trail.

Suddenly a terrifying thing happened. There was a great roar, a crack, a tearing, breaking sound, like thunder and cannons booming and echoing round the canyon. Martha was caught in a hurricane and lifted high off her feet. She was whirled round and round in the air, being struck many times by flying branches and bits of rock and showers of earth. She was turned and twisted this way and that. She was battered and bruised and filled with uncomprehending fear. Then, mercifully, she lost consciousness.

When she awoke it was night and there were stars shining above. The gun had saved her. It was still slung round her shoulders and it had wedged itself and her in the branches of an alder bush near the top of the canyon. Below her was a sheer drop, down, down to the very bottom of the canyon. She was bruised and cut, her mouth tasted of blood, and her head hurt terribly. For a while she did not understand where she was nor how dangerously she was hanging. Slowly she realised.

Then she moved her left hand a little and held on tightly to a branch. She began to shout,

"Help! Help! Don, come and help me!" There was no one who could possibly hear, but she screamed and yelled until she became unconscious again. When she awoke the next time there were still stars shining above her. Were they the same stars? Was it the same night? Or was it another night?

Everything was quiet and still, and now she became aware, painfully aware, of her bruised and broken body. Her right arm hurt with any tiny movement. Her right leg had no feeling at all. There was a frightening pain in her head, and blood had run down from it on to her face. Her face was sticky with blood. She felt afraid and desperately alone and helpless. She was filled with panic and she called and screamed again.

"Don! Come and help me! Don, come, please, please come and help me! Don! Help! Help!" Her voice, shrill and unreal, echoed round the canyon. Then as the sound died away, she heard Don's voice,

"Martha, come up here. Try to climb up to me." She knew afterwards that it could not possibly have been Don's voice, but at the time she believed that it was. He seemed to be calling to her very quietly from above.

"Try Martha, try."

She tried. Somehow she struggled out of the gun sling. Somehow she strained and stretched in the darkness, feeling for other alder branches, working her way slowly and painfully up and up the canyon wall. With one good arm and one good foot she progressed bit by bit. She dared not look down, for a slip would mean death. Panting and breathless, she stopped again and again to rest.

"I'll never do it," she thought, but then she would hear Don's voice calling and guiding her, urging her to keep on trying. Unbelievably, she managed to creep up and up until she was out of the canyon and on to solid earth at the top. Then she slept.

When she awoke, huddled up in the mud on the hill trail, she was thirsty, terribly, unbearably thirsty. She drank from a small puddle.

"I must get to the cabin," she thought. She could not walk. She could not even crawl properly. She could only lie face downwards on the ground and pull herself along with her good arm and her good leg, creeping, wriggling, moving as a worm might move. She rested often, and drank from every puddle. She dragged herself round trees, over grass and small hillocks and through mud, until at last she reached the cabin. She knew her right arm was broken, and probably her leg too. Her head hurt terribly, and blood was still flowing from her nose. She crept into the cabin and pulled the door shut. The sun was shining now. She leaned against the cabin wall and slept again.

Later in the day she worked on her right arm with her left hand. She felt and pressed and pushed at the broken place and somehow, suddenly, it clicked back into position. She found a piece of thin board and split it in two to make a splint. She bound the splint to her arm with towels and tea-cloths. She made a fire with the wood shavings and logs that were always left ready. She managed to pull her left boot off, but her right leg was so swollen and painful that she could not do anything about that boot. She realised that she was very dirty – caked with mud and dried blood. She heated some water on the fire and managed feebly to wash her face and neck. She could not do much about her hair. Chunks of it came away in her hand and the rest was matted together with blood.

With great effort and frequent rests she cut most of her clothes off with a knife. She found one of Don's big vests and struggled into it. She was tired, so tired, but much too weak to scramble on to her comfortable bunk. Her head ached unbearably and the pain in her leg frightened her. Everything seemed to sway round her. She stayed on the floor and leaned against the wall again and slept. She slept and woke and slept and woke. Sometimes when she opened her eyes she would see that it was daytime. Sometimes she would see that it was night. She lost all count of days and nights and time.

Then one day she awoke and felt hungry. Fortunately the cabin was always well-stocked with food. She ate raw oatmeal and raisins and dried apples and peanut butter. She made some tea and drank it, very hot and sweet, and felt a little better. Painfully, slowly, she at last climbed on to her bunk, wrapped herself in her eiderdown and slept again. During the night she awoke and she lay there feeling thankful that her wounds were hurting a little less. Then she felt her baby moving within her – a faint gentle movement. All this time, with the pain and the fear and the anxiety, she had not once thought of the baby. It could have been killed. It could so easily have been killed, but it was living. She rejoiced and murmured a prayer of thank-fulness.

"I must get well and strong," she thought. "I must look after the child and keep it safe."

.   .   .   .   .   .

With the storm and the hurricane had been a landslide. A great piece of the mountain had broken off and gone leaping and roaring into the depths of the canyon. Earth and boulders and bushes and rocks and trees had gone with it, half filling the canyon and quite changing the familiar landscape. The entrance to the mining tunnel had been buried deeply under rocks and earth. No one would ever be able to get to it again. Don and Sam's mine and its gleaming gold-bearing ore had gone for ever.

Meanwhile, Lloyd was beginning to get anxious about his parents. They should have been back in town days ago. The journey by boat should take only thirty-one hours or a little more. Every evening he ran down to the harbour to see if they had arrived. He made enquiries at each boat that came in, but he heard no news. The Smiths tried to cheer him,

"Your Dad told us he once took twenty-seven days on that same trip," Mr Smith reminded him.

"Yes. It was stormy then and he had to lie up in one of the creeks."

"That may be happening now. Don't worry Lloyd. They won't take any chances."

About this time, Martha began to write a diary. She had to write it with her left hand. She thought it would keep her sane and help her to sort out the tangle of confused thoughts and anxieties in her mind. She thought it would help her also to keep count of the days. She wrote of the way that she made a crutch with a broom and made it the right length by burning a piece of the handle off in the fire. She made a splint for her injured leg and a most ingenious, removable cement cast to protect her broken arm. She wrote of the jobs she did around the cabin, of shuffling around outside, bringing in branches and keeping the water-pots full before the water-hole should freeze. Every day she cut some wood shavings so that there was always a supply close at hand. She wrote of the pain in her body and most of all in her head. She wrote of Don.

"Why hasn't he come?" she asked. "Perhaps he too was caught in the landslide and is lying dead at the bottom of the canyon, or perhaps his little boat was wrecked and he was drowned."

Then there was the thought of the baby. When Lloyd

had been born, Martha had been in her mother's home in America. She had been nursed and fussed over and doped a little and had known almost nothing about it. She had never seen even a dog or a cat born. How would she manage all alone in this wilderness? How would she know what to do to get her child safely into the world?

Soon, as days and weeks went by, she realised that no one would ever come before the spring. She would be here the whole winter alone. She would have no one to help her. There were times when she felt desperate with loneliness and anxiety but she had been brought up in a religious household, and she prayed for strength and courage now.

Meanwhile the pain of her injuries became slowly less and she began day by day to feel better. She began to feel sure that Don must be safe somewhere. She felt grateful for the warm cabin and the stock of food, and the fact that the winter was milder than usual, and the snow late in coming. It did not come till December, and then she rejoiced in its beauty as it turned every tree and bush and rock to glistening white.

She wrote of the preparations she was making for the baby. She cut up some of Don's underwear to make nappies. She washed a sugar sack and soaked it till it was soft. Then she filled it with moss that she had brought into the cabin before the snow came, and she made a little mattress. She sewed it across and across to keep the moss in place with a quilted effect. She cut up a petticoat of her own and made a little frock and embroidered a tiny border with red wool, pulled out from the top of a sock. She was sure the baby would be a girl. Don wanted a daughter. Lloyd wanted a sister. It would be a girl and she would call it Donnas.

Christmas Day came. Martha, of course, could not be sure which was really Christmas Day, but she knew her calculations could not be too far wrong. She made herself a cake and some biscuits and candy. She brought a little spruce tree into the cabin and trimmed it with curls of blue paper from a macaroni box and coloured shapes cut from a magazine. She put it in a can of earth and stood it in the middle of the table. She made a tiny sock to hang up for the unborn baby. She filled it with raisins and candy and she decorated the cabin with branches of hemlock and cedar. For her dinner she had salt deer meat from the store under the floor and she fried some dried apples. She felt calm and thankful. She was nearly well, and her child was growing and moving. She sang carols, all the carols she could remember – Hark the herald angels sing, Silent night, Oh come all ye faithful, and last of all, the one that seemed most suitable of all,

"Away in a manger,
No crib for a bed,
The little Lord Jesus
Laid down His sweet head."

Now it snowed day after day – big, soft flakes that packed steadily – two metres, three metres deep. The back windows were white, and the front windows were half blocked too. With the help of her crutch, Martha stumbled and shuffled towards the water hole, but she could not find it. Water for use in the cabin now had to be melted snow.

It went on snowing – four metres deep, five metres, perhaps more. Then there was fog and sleet, and the sleet froze so that the wilderness was covered in a sheet of ice – slippery, so slippery. It gave Martha an idea, a dangerous, brilliant idea. She could sit at the top of the hill trail and slide down and down to the beach cabin. She was filled with excitement. The trail was very steep. It might be blocked in places by snow drifts. Once she started, she would not be able to turn back, but she had a great urge to go, whatever the difficulties might be. She *must* go to the beach cabin. She did not know why. Perhaps she felt there might be more chance of being rescued there. Don's gun was buried in the canyon, but there was another gun in the beach cabin. If she saw a boat, she could fire the gun to draw attention to herself. Perhaps she knew too that the snow would not be so deep down there – only half as deep perhaps.

The beach cabin was not so well equipped as the

upper cabin, so she planned to take as many things as possible with her. In a fever of activity she piled food, wood shavings, bedding, pots and pans, a tub and a saw into sacks, or rolled them up in canvas and tied them up with fuse wire. She made many journeys taking the bundles to the top of the hill trail and leaving them tied to a bush till the next day.

Early the next morning she put the splint on her leg and the cement cast on her arm. She carried her eider-down in a rucksack on her back. She tied all the bundles together in the manner of a freight train, and the last one to herself. She was just trying to push her crutch under the wire that tied the last bundle when she slid forward unexpectedly. Part of the bush snapped off and everything began to slide forwards. She grabbed at another bush, missed it, and found herself careering downhill. The snow was hard and icy with a few snow-drifts to negotiate. She only just missed a tree or two,

and on she flew and was at the bottom of the trail in scarcely more than a single breath. She stopped within an easy distance of the beach cabin door. It was wonderful! She was at the cabin before she had even meant to start. She sat still and laughed aloud.

. . . .

The baby was born in February. It was a girl with dark, soft hair sticking up all over her head. She was a beautiful child, small and pink and neatly rounded. Donnas had come. At home, she would have been carried to the church and christened. Martha decided that she would conduct a christening service herself, here by the sea. And who would be the guests? Deer — forty or fifty starving deer, who were wandering on the beach searching among the broken ice for scraps of seaweed.

"I'll bake some bread for you," promised Martha. "You shall come to our christening feast and share our food and our happiness."

A week or two later the christening took place. Donnas was dressed in her best and wrapped in a blanket. Martha called to the deer and walked to the edge of the sea. She had been to many christenings and could remember parts of the service. She turned to the deer and began,

"Dearly beloved, we are gathered here in the sight of God –" and on till she came to "Donnas Martin, I baptise thee in the name of the Father, and of the Son and of the Holy Ghost. Amen." She knelt by the sea and dipped her fingers in the icy water and made the sign of the cross on the baby.

Then she scattered her homemade bread among the deer. Some stayed at a distance, but some came near and nearer, and two or three took food from her hand. A thrush came too and shared the feast, and a small flock of little tits fluttered round from the nearby bushes.

. . . .

There was only one piece of paper left to write upon. Martha would have to do very small, small writing. It did not matter too much now. She had no longer the need to write of her sufferings and her sorrow. She was no longer lonely. She had her baby. She had faith that someone would come soon and rescue her. A prospector might come, searching for gold. A fisherman might anchor his boat in the bay. A bear hunter might come. Someone would surely come soon.

There had been a great storm and the sea-ice had broken up and drifted away from the shore. Seven grey arctic geese had taken shelter outside the cabin door. Blueberry blossoms were opening on the bushes and the sun had a touch of spring warmth about it.

Martha looked up and saw two Indian canoes out in the bay. She picked up her gun and fired it. She shouted. She waved. The Indians saw her. There were nineteen of them, men and women and small shy children. They were on their way to one of their fishing grounds, where they would find herrings. It had been a bad winter for them. They needed the herrings

badly, but they turned their canoes and paddled them towards the shore, towards Martha and her baby.

.   .   .   .   .   .

Martha wrote no more, so we can only imagine the reunion with Don, for he too was safe. After meeting the mailboat and starting the return journey, his outboard motor had failed. A trapper had come along and towed him further. The trapper's boat was full of supplies for the winter, but it too, had run into trouble as the storm had blown up. The two men had been wrecked on an island. There, after a while, they had repaired the boat and worked their way gradually from island to island until they had reached a fairly safe shelter. Then snow and ice had trapped them for the rest of the winter and it was not until spring that they were able to get away, with better weather and a homemade sail.

So Martha and Don and Lloyd came together again, and baby Donnas was welcomed and cuddled and loved and admired as much as any baby had ever been.

Based on *O Rugged Land of Gold* by Martha Martin. Copyright 1953 by Macmillan Publishing Co Inc, renewed 1981 by Christina H. Niemi. Adaptation used by permission of Macmillan Publishing Co Inc.

The Valley of the Kings

Many of the ancient pharaohs of Egypt lie sleeping in the Valley of the Kings. Their mummified bodies are entombed in the rock, accompanied by an incredible assortment of treasures from their earthly life, and by some of the objects they may need in their afterlife. They have not, alas, always slept in peace. Most of the tombs have at some time been disturbed and robbed, first by tomb robbers for greed, then sometimes by priests for protection, then by excavators for the benefit of museums, and finally by archaeologists for the sake of knowledge and history.

To the Valley of the Kings in 1917 came two English men, Lord Carnarvon and Howard Carter. They had received permission from the Egyptian government to dig and excavate in an attempt to find more things of interest. Over the years about sixty tombs had been discovered in rooms tunnelled into the rock, behind doors hidden by centuries of shifting sand. There surely could not be any more to find. Surely the Valley of the Kings must already have yielded up all its secrets. Many historians thought this must be so, but Carnarvon and Carter were filled with the necessary optimism of all explorers and archaeologists.

Carter in fact had a specific hope and ambition. There was one king whose burial place had never been found – a king called Tutankhamun about whom very little was known. Carter had a few clues to follow, but chiefly he followed his own particular conviction and a sort of scholarly instinct.

He had started his working life as a draughtsman and had been employed in the British Museum inking in traced sketches of Egyptian tombs. He was so careful and thorough, and so interested in the subject that the following year he was taken to Egypt with an archaeological group. Within a few more years he had risen to be an expert in the field. Then he was put in touch with Lord Carnarvon, whose introduction to Egypt had been rather different.

He was a wealthy man with a stately home in Berkshire. He was interested in antiques and old drawings. He was keen on sport and had been round the world on a sailing ship. Then as early cars took to the roads he became an enthusiastic racing motorist. This resulted in an accident in which he was badly hurt and which made his breathing difficult for the rest of his life. No longer was he able to take part in any active sport, or even to remain in the cold, damp English climate during the winter. He chose therefore to go to Egypt, where he became intensely interested in its history and its art and in the activities of various groups sifting the sands in the Valley of the Kings. It is said that when one door closes in life, another opens. So it was now with Carnarvon. One door closed on sport. Another opened on Egyptian archaeology. He had the money. He had the time. He had the interest. All he needed was an expert to guide him. He chose Howard Carter.

There were always plenty of local men willing to be hired as diggers. They did it well. After all they had been doing it, on and off, for a very long time. Under Carter's direction and in Carnarvon's pay, a team began to work in about the middle of the Valley of the Kings. There had been so many excavating parties before, that the sand was strewn with bits of rock and piles of rubble. There had been no real system, and there were no plans or proper records of what had been done.

Carter worked in a very different way, methodically and systematically digging down through the sand.

During the first season he removed layers and layers of rubble and layers and layers of sand until he came to some flint boulders and the remains of some ancient huts used by long-dead workmen. He soon found that his work was getting in the way of tourists who came in large numbers to visit the tomb of Rameses VI near by, so he decided to move further along the valley.

For five seasons the Carnarvon-Carter team worked, patiently digging and searching with very little result. Carnarvon was beginning to give up hope, and when he returned home to England at the end of the fifth season, he decided to pour no more money into what seemed a fruitless venture. He sent for Carter in order to break the news to him.

"I'm giving up," he said. "I feel it's no good wasting any more money."

"Oh don't say that," replied Carter despondently.

"Well," continued Carnarvon, "you must admit that we've had somewhat scanty results, and last season was more depressing than usual. Do you know we've removed 200 000 tonnes of rubble and sand and we haven't found a single object of any importance?"

"True," agreed Carter, "but let's try for one more season." He unrolled a map of the valley and pointed to the entrance to the tomb of Rameses VI. "I've a feeling we ought to try again here," he said, "where we were digging in the first season."

"Yes, but we moved from there because we were obstructing the tourists."

"We could start earlier in the season before too many tourists come. There's a patch there that we didn't investigate fully. You remember the place where we found those old workmen's huts and flint boulders? I feel we ought to dig below them."

"Mm," nodded Carnarvon without enthusiasm.

"Look here," went on Carter eagerly. "If we don't get any results next season, I'll bear the cost of the labourers myself."

Carnarvon was touched by this offer.

"All right," he agreed. "We'll dig for one more winter and I'll finance it as before, but we'll make this the very last season."

"Unless we find something, of course."

"Of course."

Carter rolled up his map and sighed with relief. He would have been most unhappy to leave the work unfinished.

On October the twenty-eighth 1922 he was back in Egypt. He wanted to give as little trouble as possible to the tourists, and if he started digging at once he might get most of his rubble out of the way before they arrived. He assembled his labourers and on November the first they started taking down the workmen's huts which had been standing there since 1150 B.C. after the making of the tomb of Rameses VI. When the first hut was down and a trench was dug below it, there came an exciting moment. A step was revealed, cut in the rock, and in the following days another and another – a whole flight of steps – leading where?

The steps descended below the valley floor and below the level of the entrance to the tomb of Rameses VI. Quite obviously this must be the entrance to

another tomb, but whose tomb? It might be that of a priest or some lesser person. And if indeed it was the hoped-for tomb of a king, it might already have been robbed and stripped of its contents in the days of antiquity. Howard Carter could not conceal his excitement, and the Egyptian workmen were as elated and anxious as he was. By November the fifth enough rubble had been cleared away to expose the twelfth step, and at that level the upper part of a door became visible. A door! It was closed and plastered and sealed with the seal of the royal cemetery guards. This was proof that the tomb must be that of a person of great importance. It meant too, that it could not have been plundered for three thousand years.

Carter wished fervently that Lord Carnarvon had been with him to share the thrill of this moment and he felt that it was only fair to delay any further exploration until Carnarvon could return to Egypt to join him. On the morning of the next day he sent a telegram to him – a telegram that has gone down in history.

"At last have made wonderful discovery in valley; a magnificent tomb with seals intact; re-covered same for your arrival."

Loyally he resisted the temptation to ask his men to dig further. In fact he directed them to replace the

sand and rubble and to conceal the door and the stairway and then to take turns with him in guarding the spot. Travel was a fairly slow business in those days, and Lord Carnarvon did not arrive until the twenty-third, so Carter had nearly three weeks in which to hope and wonder – Whose tomb was it? Was it that of a king? Was the king Tutankhamun?

By November the twenty-fourth the entire stairway was cleared. There were sixteen steps in all, and now that the whole of the door was exposed it could be seen that other seals had been impressed upon the plaster. These were the seals of Tutankhamun himself. This, at last, must be Tutankhamun's tomb!

The thrill of finding the royal seals however was somewhat tempered by the discovery that part of the door had, in fact, been opened and closed again. Thieves had at some time entered the tomb. However they could not have taken a great deal out otherwise the cemetery guards would not have taken the trouble to re-seal the door and block the stairway. Certainly no one had seen the tomb since Rameses VI had died.

The door led to a passage descending further into the rock. It was filled with rubble and stones and broken pots and water skins. The workers had to clear it rather slowly because some of the objects, though small, were of value. It was the middle of the afternoon of November the twenty-sixth before a second door was reached, nine metres lower than the first. This too bore impressions of the seal of the royal cemetery guards and the seal of Tutankhamun. What was behind it? With trembling hands, Carter prepared to look. This was the most wonderful day of his life, his "day of days" as he called it, and with him to share it were Lord Carnarvon and his daughter and an eminent egyptologist named Callender.

Carter cut a small opening in the upper left-hand corner of the door and pushed an iron rod through to feel what was beyond. There was no rubble here. There was space. He now held a lighted candle against the hole to make sure that there were no poisonous gases. Then he cut the hole a little bigger. He held the candle inside it, and peered through, with his three companions waiting impatiently to hear what he could observe. No words can describe the wonder of the next few moments better than the words of Carter himself,

"At first I could see nothing, the hot air escaping from the chamber causing the candle flame to flicker, but presently as my eyes grew accustomed to the light, details of the room within emerged slowly from the mist, strange animals, statues and gold – everywhere the glint of gold. For the moment – an eternity it must have seemed to the others standing by – I was struck dumb with amazement, and when Lord Carnarvon, unable to stand the suspense any longer, inquired anxiously, 'Can you see anything?' it was all I could do to get out the words, 'Yes, wonderful things.'"

Wonderful things! There were indeed wonderful things all jumbled up together in an incredible state of disarray, leaning against each other, piled on top of each other like a giant version of the contents of a child's toy box emptied carelessly on to the floor. There were four chariots that had been dismantled in order to get them through the doors. There were three beds in the shape of elongated animals, whose fantastic golden heads threw strange, unreal shadows on the

wall. There was an unbelievably beautiful throne inlaid with brilliant patterns of semi-precious stones and coloured glass paste. There were exquisitely carved seats and stools and chairs.

There were caskets and boxes made of gold and reeds and ivory. There were daggers and staves and weapons, trumpets and vases and pots and baskets. There were robes and sandals spilling out of painted chests. There were strings of beads and cases of rings. There were objects of turquoise and gold and alabaster and ebony and lapis-lazuli. There was a great gilded snake rearing its head out of a container. The display was dazzling, gleaming, and though it had obviously been disarranged by robbers who had been disturbed, it had nevertheless been lying there in all its wonder and beauty for more than three thousand years.

One thing was missing. There was nothing resembling a coffin. There was no mummy. But at the far side of the room were two lifesize statues of the king. They were varnished in shining black and they wore kilt-like loin cloths and sandals all of gold. They stood facing each other and guarding yet another sealed door. On the other side of this door surely, would be the embalmed body of Tutankhamun.

. . . . . .

The amount of work that faced Carter now was formidable. With admirable restraint he decided that all these objects must be catalogued, photographed, given preservative treatment and moved to a place of safety before the further door was opened. So it was not until February the seventeenth 1923 that this took place, disclosing an enormous, brilliant shrine of gilded wood. This shrine contained a second shrine. The second contained a third, and the third contained a fourth. All were of gilded wood, and the fourth one contained a heavy rectangular coffin of quartzite. This contained three more coffins in the shape of beautifully decorated mummies, one inside the other. The last of them was made of solid gold, and it exposed to sight what might be considered the most beautiful of all the wonderful examples of ancient craftsmanship in the tomb. It was a death mask created in faithful likeness of the king. It was made of polished gold inlaid with coloured glass paste and semi-precious stones. After more than three thousand years it still gleamed and shone and showed Tutankhamun as he appeared in life – young, gentle, serene and handsome.

This innermost coffin was not opened until October the twenty-eighth 1925 because of various delays and disagreements between Carter and the Egyptian government. Then, amid a group of eminent egyptologists the wrappings were unwound, revealing more than a hundred and forty gold jewels in different places and at last the body of the king with a tiny wreath of withered flowers, still faintly tinted with colour and botanically recognisable.

Sadly, Lord Carnarvon was not there to witness this last of secrets, for he had died in 1923, four months after the discovery of the tomb in the Valley of the Kings. His death had been caused by a mosquito bite leading to blood poisoning and pneumonia. There was nothing sinister about it, but it was reported and embellished, and was declared (by someone unknown) to be due to the "curse of the pharaohs".

The newspapers had of course spread the news of the discovery of the treasure of Tutankhamun, and people in many countries had been following every development with interest. There were many who regarded the excavators' work as a service to history, but there were also many who regarded it as an intrusion upon the sanctity of the grave. There never had been a "curse of the pharaohs" but the newspapers regarded the idea as a good story. For years, off and on, they exploited it to the full. Anyone who died after being even remotely connected with the disturbing of the tomb was said to have been a victim of the "curse of the pharaohs". At least twenty-one "victims" were given this news treatment though many died long afterwards. Some died from complaints developed earlier and most died in old age.

Carter spent his next ten years sorting, studying and listing the precious objects and writing three books on the subject. In a way he had brought Tutankhamun to life, but even so, very little is known about the boy king. He was married to a princess at the age of nine and became king at the same time, somewhere about 1360 years before the birth of Christ. His reign was pathetically brief, for examination of his mummy indicated that he was only eighteen when he died. He had not been king long enough to do anything of note. Why then was he buried with such indescribable splendour? Why was he surrounded by treasures so much greater in number and value than other much more famous pharaohs whose tombs had been found? Why had this boy king been entombed in such glory and then so soon forgotten? The question cannot really be answered.

Most of the treasures are now in the Cairo Museum – two whole galleries of them. But Tutankhamun, with all awe and reverence, was laid to rest again in his original tomb in the Valley of the Kings.

The Bell Rock

Seventeen kilometres from the east coast of Scotland lies the Bell Rock, or the Inchcape Rock as it used to be called. It rises in the cold North Sea, wild, stormy, fraught with danger. It is hardly ever entirely dry, and for most of the time it is hidden by the tide. Then, invisible and totally submerged, it becomes more of a menace than ever to passing ships. Many have been wrecked on it through the centuries, and many sailors have lost their lives.

The nearest port to it is Arbroath and here, from times long past, is a monastery. At one time, some of the monks went out in a small boat and managed to fix a bell on the rock. Perhaps in those days an odd tree clung to life there or perhaps the monks were able to fix the bell to a jagged point of rock or perhaps to an anchored float. As the waves swirled about it, the bell rang, giving a low warning that echoed across the stormy sea for a considerable distance. Whether it had any effect during the hours when it was deeply submerged is doubtful, but it must have saved many lives.

The poet Robert Southey wrote a poem about it called "The Inchcape Rock". In it he told the story of Ralph the Rover, a pirate who cut the bell down, intending to plunder ships that would be wrecked there. The scheme brought about his downfall however, as some time later his own ship drifted in those waters in a thick mist with no bell to guide it,

"... the vessel strikes with a shivering shock –
Oh heaven! It is the Inchcape Rock!"
This may be just a story, but certainly at some time the bell was washed away and not replaced.

In 1793 the Northern Lighthouse Trust of Scotland talked of putting a light on Bell Rock, as it was usually called then. A lighthouse was needed desperately, and vague plans were considered. As the rock was so often under water it was obvious that the difficulties, and therefore the financial burden, would be enormous, and the plan was abandoned.

Four years later, the winter in that part of Scotland was so stormy that more than seventy ships went down in a single week. If there had been a light on the dreaded rock, many of the ships and lives might have been saved. The people became very angry about all these tragedies and they asked repeatedly that a light should be placed on Bell Rock. Two public-spirited men actually put simple lights there themselves, but the storms that followed soon washed them away. The Northern Lighthouse Trust of Scotland felt that the only possible solution would be a lighthouse on a strongly-built stone tower, but there certainly was not enough money for this.

Then into the story came Robert Stevenson. He was a lighthouse engineer who had learned patience and courage while building, inspecting and repairing lighthouses in conditions of great danger and dis-comfort. He was a kind, compassionate man, who did everything he could to help lighthouse keepers and lighthouse builders and to make their lives as comfort-able as possible in the very *un*comfortable conditions in which they had to live and work.

He knew that it would be a long time before the Lighthouse Trust would have enough money to build a lighthouse on Bell Rock, but he decided to prepare himself for the possibility. He twice visited a light-house in Ireland while it was being built on a similar sea-washed foundation, and he studied a book by

Smeaton, the builder of the Eddystone Lighthouse at Plymouth. He worked out several ideas of his own, and made a number of drawings and plans. The North Sea was particularly stormy. The Bell Rock was particularly exposed to the elements as well as being submerged for much of the time. It would need a very special lighthouse, built in a very special way.

He thought and thought about it, as well as carrying on with his ordinary work and studying part-time at Edinburgh University. He thought there might not be a good enough foundation for a stone building. It might be better to build a lighthouse perched on strong iron pillars, or perhaps make a floating light of some sort. He knew that he could not take any decision on the structure until spring came and he could examine the Bell Rock himself.

When April the first came, he tried to hire a boat and a boatman to take him there, but the sea was so wild and rough that it would have been folly to attempt the voyage. It had then to be postponed until May the first, when he was to begin a tour of lighthouse inspections again. He hoped to go via the rock, but again the seas were impossible, and he could not even get within sight of it.

When he finished his tour, it was early October. In the company of an architect friend, he tried again to hire a boat to take him to the Bell Rock. The weather was good now and the tide would be at its lowest for many months. All the same, fishermen and boatmen were unwilling to risk their lives. They knew the reputation of the rock too well. At last Robert found a man who agreed to take him. He was a fisherman, but he also went to Bell Rock from time to time, searching for bits of wreckage – useful pieces of wood or sometimes coins or small things of value. He explained that it would be possible to stay on the rock for two hours only. So the three men crossed the tossing sea and reached the rock. A colony of seals barked a welcome, or perhaps a warning, and some of them slid down into the water, diving and swimming happily enough in the roaring breakers and the shoals of fish.

Robert Stevenson had feared this moment but had longed for it too. Now at last he was standing on the treacherous Bell Rock. Now he had only two hours in which to examine it. He had only two hours to decide about a floating light or a light fixed on iron pillars or a stone tower built on the rock. He realised very quickly that the first two would not withstand the fury of the sea, but to his delight he saw that there were solid, strong, and reasonably level places which would provide good foundations for a stone tower. This then was his decision – a tall, circular lighthouse tower built of stone.

It was many years before he was given permission to start building. Parliament had to approve the spending of the large sum of money needed. The Northern Light-house Trust had to approve Robert's plans. Many people thought the whole idea would prove to be impossible, but no one took the risk of going out to view the rock for himself.

Meanwhile Robert realised that a great deal of time was going to be wasted ferrying workmen back and forth to the rock. He suggested that they should live on a ship anchored near it, and that later they might build for themselves a sort of cabin on legs on the rock itself. He suggested too that the temporary wooden tower should be used to hold a light and save lives while the lighthouse was being built. This would mean also that extra shipping dues could be charged to ships, and the money collected at the ports could be put towards the expenses of the building.

There were many difficulties and differences of opinion to be overcome, and Robert visited several Scottish quarries to find the most suitable type of stone to use. He chose granite, which had to be transported in huge blocks to a workyard set up at the little port of Arbroath on the mainland. Cranes and tools and piles of cement were sent to Arbroath too; and more than a hundred workmen arrived – masons, plumbers, carpenters, labourers, workers of all kinds. Some of them brought their wives and children, so that the quiet little fishing port was suddenly swamped with sheds and storehouses, people, noise and industry. The task of working out all the details of the project would have dismayed a weaker man than Robert Stevenson, but even he sometimes felt overwhelmed by the heavy responsibilities that burdened him.

As the tower was to be circular and decreasing in girth as it rose, each stone had to be differently and separately cut and prepared before it left Arbroath. Each stone had to be dovetailed on each side so that it

would fit into the stone above, below, and left and right, like a huge, complicated jigsaw puzzle. Robert had therefore to discuss the working and shaping of each stone with the masons. Thousands of stone blocks would eventually be used and he could not afford a single mistake.

Then there was the supervision of the boat in which the workmen would sleep. The one chosen was re-named *Pharos* (a Greek word meaning "lighthouse"). She had three masts on which lights and reflectors were fixed. She was fitted up with thirty bunks, and a specially-designed anchor to hold her in position near the rock. There was also a supply boat called *Smeaton* which was to bring materials from Arbroath and to ferry the men back and forth from the *Pharos* to the rock or the mainland as necessary.

One of Robert's hardest tasks now was to persuade enough workmen to join him for the first shift. Two of them fled at the very mention of Bell Rock. Its dangers had been well known for centuries, and men would have to battle with sheer fear as well as with other trials like sea-sickness and the worry of leaving wives and children. At last, however, enough men had been signed on for the first shift of a month or two, so on August the seventeenth in the year 1807 they all attended a church service. Then at ten o'clock in the evening they sailed out of Arbroath on the *Smeaton*, cheered by many friends and relatives and sightseers.

At five o'clock next morning the *Smeaton* reached the rock and the men saw for the first time the place where many of them would be working on and off for years ahead. They saw the ship *Pharos* waiting to welcome them. They saw the notorious Bell Rock with waves crashing over it. A group of sleepy seals stared in surprise and slid and dived down into the sea from the rock that had been their undisturbed home for so long. Soon a new sound mingled with the roar of the breakers, the barking of the seals and the cry of seabirds. It was the sound of hammers and pick-axes ringing and clanging and echoing over the rock. The building of a lighthouse on Bell Rock had begun.

. . . . . .

A routine of sorts was soon established, depending of course on the weather. At dawn each day the men usually rowed to Bell Rock from the *Pharos*. It was only a short journey, but many of them were seasick day after day and landed nervously on the rock, slippery with seaweed. Meals were cooked on the *Pharos* and sent across to the working site. Winter work would be impossible, so every moment of daylight and favourable tide had to be used.

The most important thing to Robert was the safety and comfort of his workers, so the first thing he organised was the erection of a wooden beacon tower to hold a light and to provide a high platform where men could clamber out of reach of the sea if they were stranded at all.

In the past any wooden beacon had been washed away almost at once, so Robert had planned his very carefully. He asked the men to chisel six deep holes for the legs. These were fifteen metres long and made of wood. They fitted into iron sockets in the holes in the rock and they rose into a sort of rough pyramid. A light was put on the top, and the platform was fixed between the struts and equipped with fresh water and a tin of biscuits.

This simple structure gave more confidence to the men. If they were stranded, there would be somewhere to go out of the reach of the sea! It also provided a dry place for the blacksmith to work on his forge.

Specially-built barges brought the huge stones from Arbroath. Cranes and winches lifted them ashore, and a specially-built, raised, iron railway carried them to the site. Meanwhile men were now at work hacking away a large circular hole in the rock where the foundations were to be laid. Only twice a day at low tide could they work in any sort of comfort. During the rest of the hours of daylight the tide was creeping up and up, and the icy water was washing round their ankles, their knees, their waists.

All the men admired and respected Robert. He was usually first on the rock in the morning and always last away from it in the evening. He looked after them in every way, and when occasionally an accident happened to one of them, or a man became ill, he would make sure that his wife and children were well cared for. He must often have longed to spend more time with his own wife and children at home in Edinburgh, but as long as men were working on Bell Rock he was working there with them, sharing the dangers and the discomforts.

The men who had started out with such fears and misgivings became such keen and loyal workers that Robert now found it hard to keep them away from the work, for they would often carry on in the evening by the light of flickering torches. Other men from the mainland heard such good reports of the project that they became willing, even eager, to join the team or to take the place of any member of it who had to go home for a while. It became a matter of pride in Scotland to say, "I'm building the lighthouse on Bell Rock."

At the end of October the lower part of the beacon legs were coated with pitch, and then work had to stop until the spring. The *Smeaton* took the workers back to Arbroath, and only the crew of the *Pharos* stayed on duty during the winter, with the lights on its masts swaying and gleaming in the mists and storms.

In May 1808 Bell Rock was again a scene of feverish activity. The *Pharos* and the *Smeaton* had been made more comfortable, and another boat, the *Sir Joseph Banks*, provided more accommodation. The two most important jobs now were the deepening of the pit for the lighthouse foundations, and the conversion of the beacon platform into a strange, secure little cabin reached by a rope ladder. It was painted outside with tar, and lined inside with moss, and it provided many of the men with comfortable bunks and did away with the daily journeys to and from the ships.

In July the first stone foundation was laid with some ceremony, and by August the twelfth, the last stone of

the base completed the first layer of the lighthouse tower. The stones fitted into each other perfectly and were kept in place by long spikes. There were a hundred and twenty-three stones. They weighed a hundred and four tonnes.

Slowly, layer by layer, course by course, the stone tower began to rise on the rock. This thrilled the workers. They could now actually watch the lighthouse growing and taking shape. It was lashed continuously by furious waves so that the mortar was often washed away before it could dry. Sea water had to be pumped out at every stage of the work, and as fast as the tower rose, it was swamped and submerged twice a day and hidden by the tides.

On April the thirtieth 1809, the third season began. The rock was white with snow, and seals had taken up residence again. Limpets clung to the legs of the beacon cabin, and seaweed trailed and twisted itself round them. Cormorants and gulls had even made nests in the corners of its supports and struts – but it was safe. It was still standing, firm and strong. The men returned to their work. The seals slipped noisily away. Seabirds shrieked their protests. The tower began to rise, stone by stone, course by course. Before this, the men had worked with water swirling round them. Now as the tower grew higher and higher there was the new hazard of being blown off it by violent winds.

Year by year, season by season, the tower grew taller, one course upon another, becoming narrower and narrower as it rose. Floors, ceilings, rooms, spiral staircases were fitted inside. Danger was always there. Storms returned and returned.

At last the stone work was completed. The light room was built on the tower. The oil-fed lantern was put in place. The light mechanism was fixed up so that the light would revolve every three minutes, and in misty weather two bells could be set ringing. Once more the Inchcape Rock had a bell, and on the evening of February the first 1811, Robert Stevenson's light-

house on Bell Rock sent a bright shaft of light flashing across the sea.

. . . . . .

Robert's story is only part of the history of the Stevenson family as a whole. Eight of the men were lighthouse builders over five generations. Robert alone provided eighteen of Scotland's lighthouses, and other members of the family added over seventy more. In addition to these, they built bridges, buoys, roads, harbour lights and fog signals. They travelled widely and designed lighthouses for places as far away as China, Japan, India, Australia. Every lighthouse in the world owes something to the skill and industry of this amazing family. The Stevensons made life for every sailor, every voyager, better and safer.

. . . . . .

You have probably heard of Robert Louis Stevenson. You may have read some of his books – *Treasure Island*, *Kidnapped*, *The Black Arrow*, *Doctor Jekyll and Mr Hyde*, and some of his poems for children. He was the grandson of Robert, the builder of Bell Rock lighthouse. He too was trained to be a lighthouse builder like his grandfather, his father, his uncles and cousins but his health was so bad that he had to give up the idea. Instead he turned more and more to writing, dreaming up stories of danger and action and adventure in which he would have loved to take part, and in which his relatives had so often lived.

Adapted from the book *A Star for Seamen*, by
Craig Mair, published by John Murray

Fly, Elizabeth

As a very young child, Elizabeth Barrett was making rhymes over her bread and milk, so that her parents must have realised early that she was a poet born, or if not a poet, at least a most intelligent and unusual little girl. Life was kind to Elizabeth in childhood. Eldest of a family of eleven (three girls and eight boys) she grew up in a house set in a large garden where fruit trees and horse-chestnuts scattered their blossoms for her delight, and where, beyond the gate, sunny meadows and deep, damp woods stretched away to the Malvern Hills.

The house was called Hope End, from early English words meaning "house at the end of the hidden valley" which indeed it was. Edward Moulton Barrett, the father, had converted the house to stables and had had a new house built beside it in a strange Turkish style

with archways and domes and minarets "crowned with metal spires and crescents". These decorations filled Elizabeth with fear because she had heard neighbours say that they would attract "every lightning of heaven". Once, in fact, during a terrible storm she thought the house had certainly been struck, but realised afterwards that only a tree near the windows had been damaged. This was fearful enough, "the bark rent from top to bottom" as she wrote long afterwards, "– torn into long ribbons by the dreadful fiery hands – The whole trunk of that tree was bared and peeled – and up that new whiteness of it ran the finger-mark of the lightning in a bright beautiful rose-colour – the fever-sign of the certain death".

Apart from the fear of storms and the awful example of the stricken tree daily visible, the children loved Hope End and its beautiful surroundings. They had their own small gardens to tend, and plenty of exciting places to hide and play, great spreading trees to climb and a jet black pony called Moses to ride. Their mother was sweet and gentle, though much wearied by constant child-bearing. Their father was young and kind and often played with them as if he were a boy himself. He helped and advised poor people in the neighbouring town and often visited the sick. To be sure he expected instant obedience from his children, but this was the natural thing at that time and the children did not resent his attitude in the least. They loved and respected him and shared their jokes and their fun with him.

In those days of the early nineteenth century, girls were expected to sit demurely over such gentle pursuits as music and fine sewing, but Elizabeth was allowed considerable freedom in her lessons and her play, both of which she greeted with the energy and enthusiasm that were part of her character. She was very small for her age, with big, expressive eyes and dark curling hair. Although she loved romping and running and climbing with her young brothers, she also loved browsing among her father's books, daydreaming by the fire, writing majestic verses or studying Greek and Latin with her tutor. So life passed very pleasantly until she was fifteen.

Then one day she went to the paddock expecting to find Moses ready for her to ride. Just as there were servants in the house, so there were a groom and a boy in the stables. Edward Moulton Barrett was a rich man and his children, though they were taught to help others, were not expected to do much for themselves. Elizabeth thought the black pony would be saddled and waiting as he usually was at this time, and she planned to gallop and gallop across the fields until he and she were tired. There was Moses in the paddock but he was grazing freely by the fence.

"Where's your saddle?" asked Elizabeth, climbing on the gate and leaning over to stroke him. "Wait there. I'll go and get it." She went to the stable. There

was no sign of the groom or the stable boy, but the horse's saddle and bridle were hanging in their usual place. The saddle was awkward to carry but she bore it to the paddock and managed to get it in position on the pony's back. She reached under his body to fasten the straps. She struggled for a moment while Moses waited patiently. Then the saddle slipped, and in trying to save it, Elizabeth lost her balance. She clutched wildly at Moses, missed him and fell. The heavy saddle tumbled on top of her and she was aware of the terrific impact as she hit the ground. Then she knew nothing more until she opened her eyes a little later in her own bedroom.

Soon the local doctor came and said that she had injured her spine and must stay in bed for several weeks. Probably she never rode Moses again, but after a while she recovered sufficiently to drive the family pony and trap down the lanes and to take up the threads of her ordinary existence again. All the same the accident marked a definite change in her life, the change from bounding, tireless energy to quieter, more introspective ways, the change perhaps from childhood to adulthood.

. . . .

Many years passed. The family had moved several times and were now established in Wimpole Street, London.

The mother and a much-loved uncle had died long since, and Elizabeth's favourite brother had been drowned. Elizabeth had been ill many times and was now regarded as a permanent invalid. She spent her days lying on a couch in a large upstairs room and was waited on by Lily Wilson, her personal maid. Her brothers and sisters, singly or in a crowd, came up to chat with her or carried her down to join them below. Her golden spaniel, Flush, petted and pampered, shared her couch. The windows were darkened, and ivy was trained to climb across the glass. The woods, the hills, the garden at Hope End had become but a memory and Elizabeth's days were spent in reading books and writing poetry, daydreaming and making wistful plans for the time when she would be well again.

Had she lived today she would have been given treatment and light and air, but in her day she was protected from the very things she needed. The cause of her illness had become somewhat vague. Was it the fall with the horse that had started all this, or was it the chest weakness diagnosed by another doctor, or was it a nervous complaint suggested by a third? Elizabeth certainly did not know, and sadly she accepted the fact that she would never walk more than a few steps again. "A bird in a cage", she called herself, and she had been so long a prisoner that the thought of activity could now only frighten her.

Meanwhile she was making a name for herself as a poet, and had had a number of poems published. The postman kept her in touch with the literary world she loved, bringing her books and proofs, notes from editors and letters of appreciation from people who admired her work.

Then, one January evening, came a letter that lifted her to the skies. It began,

"I love your verses with all my heart, dear Miss Barrett –" This was nothing new. Many people had praised her poems. Many had written just as charmingly, but this letter was signed,

"Yours very truly,
    Robert Browning."

Not only was Elizabeth thrilled because he, a great poet himself, had stooped to notice her work, but her heart was touched too in a strange inexplicable way. Thus began a deep friendship. Elizabeth wrote back at once to thank the poet for his kindness, and letters then went backwards and forwards from his part of London to hers.

Browning wrote of books and writers. Elizabeth told of her childhood days and let her pen wander among her thoughts and dreams. Soon Browning wrote of meeting her. Could he not call one day? Elizabeth wanted to see him as much as he wished to see her, but she was shy of strangers, and vague in her reply. As a correspondent and a poet she knew that she fascinated him, but as a woman, pale and weak and lying on a couch, what feelings could she arouse in him but pity and disappointment? In February he wrote to say that it was "real warm Spring, dear Miss

Barrett" and in spring he *would* see her. Desiring, yet delaying the meeting, she replied that spring did not really come till the end of May. She kept him away through March and April. Then, at last, weakened by his persistence, she consented to admit him, explaining that he could call between two and six when Mr Barrett was out.

To call while Edward Moulton Barrett was out was essential. He was still devoted to his children, and was still full of good intentions. He had always forbidden certain of their friends to enter the house and had always tried to crush any signs of independence. He had a fanatical desire to keep his sons and daughters all under his influence even now they were grown up. He strongly resisted any thoughts of love and marriage. One of the girls, Henrietta, had planned secret meetings with young men, and there had been a most terrible scene when her father had found out about one of them. Poor Henrietta had been carried from the room in hysterics and Elizabeth had fainted with distress.

One of the brothers, Alfred, had also decided to marry, but this idea too was cruelly crushed. Love! Marriage! Not if Mr Barrett could prevent it! There is no doubt that he loved his children, particularly Elizabeth, who had always been clever and anxious to please, and who now was more surely his possession than any of the others. She most certainly was safe, lying as she did in perpetual twilight. In her helplessness she could never even think of love and marriage. Yet it was the gentle Elizabeth who was driven to defy him.

"Come between two and six, when my father is always out," she wrote to Robert Browning.

The date was fixed for May the sixteenth, and as the time drew near, Elizabeth waited in an agony of nervousness and suspense. Why had she been foolish enough to say yes? Other men had asked to see her before this, but she had always refused. Why had she not refused Robert Browning? Even now she could ring for Wilson her maid, and tell her not to admit Mr Browning, but to say that she had a headache this afternoon. Flush, the dog, barked suddenly at a sound below. There were voices and footsteps on the stairs, then a knock at the door of her room.

"Come in," said Elizabeth Barrett, and in strode Robert Browning, bringing, though neither of them saw it then, hope, and health and freedom and life itself.

Friendship seldom stands still. It either fades and dies in the early stages or else it goes forward from strength to strength as two characters unfold before each other. One meeting leads inevitably to another,

and soon Robert Browning was visiting Elizabeth, not to talk of poetry but to urge her to rebel – to rebel against closed curtains and locked windows, to rebel against doctors and the English climate, and, hardest of all, to rebel against her father.

"Plants need sun and air," said he. "You are shutting out the very things that would help to heal you. You say that you cannot walk more than a few tottering steps, but how long is it since you tried? Every day that you do not use your legs they grow weaker. Perhaps, if you tried to use them a little, and then a little more and a little more, they would grow stronger."

He begged her to make the attempt. He suggested that with the help of Wilson or one of the family she could move about from room to room, go out on sunny days in the carriage with her sisters and walk in the park. He talked of Italy, a land that he loved. H' spoke of blue skies and the health-giving sun.

"It would do you a world of good to spend the winter in Italy," he said, "and I could join you there." Elizabeth thrilled at the idea. What could be more wonderful?

Browning and thoughts of Italy inspired her. With the help of Wilson and her brothers and sisters, she frequently made perilous journeys round the house, and even into the street. She felt so ill and weary after these attempts that without the hope and encouragement of Robert and his letters she might have been tempted to give up the struggle, but increasing gradually in strength and courage she made the tremendous advance early in July of taking short walks in the park.

Now the plans for Italy began to take shape. Her doctor declared that another winter in England would kill her. She needed a brother and a sister to accompany her. Arabel declared that she would go at whatever risk. Stormie, the eldest brother, offered to go too, and George agreed to put the proposition to Father. Father however was adamant. He saw the idea in the light of a small rebellion on the part of his children. He saw Elizabeth for some strange reason suddenly reaching towards independence.

"No," said he. "If you do so it will be under my heaviest displeasure." A pall of gloom hung over the house, and the atmosphere became tense and strained.

"Rebel!" urged Browning.

"I'll still come with you," pleaded loyal Arabel.

"I'll speak to Father again," said George.

Elizabeth was torn this way and that, but she was fond of her father and had been under his rule too long to break away easily. She tried to excuse him. He acted that way because he loved her, she said. But if he loved her so deeply would he not put her health before his own wishes? He usually spent some time in her room in the evenings but now his visits were of the briefest. It was bad enough that he was angry with her, but unfair that the rest of the family should suffer too. Elizabeth meekly gave in, and reconciled herse to the thought of the damp, cold London fog that so soon would envelop Wimpole Street.

So winter came and with it a new situation, a new test for Elizabeth's courage. Robert's visits, now one a week, and his letters, now one a day, urged the greatest rebellion of all.

"Marry me," he said, in words far more poetic. "Your father will never consent, so we shall have to do it in secret. Say the day, my Elizabeth, and we will elope to Italy."

There was never any doubt about Elizabeth's desires, but as usual she delayed the reply and then the event, "If my health continues to improve – If it can be arranged – Not yet, not just yet."

All this time Edward Moulton Barrett had not been kept uninformed about Browning's visits, but had remained blissfully ignorant of their true nature. He had been proud of Elizabeth's growing reputation as a poet, and rather proud of the fact that an important man like Browning should seek her friendship and find pleasure in discussing poetry with her. That owning had any other motives, that Elizabeth, e, obedient Elizabeth, was planning despite all 's" to marry him was a possibility that simply tered his unromantic head. There was of ays the chance that he might suddenly become suspicious. Elizabeth's two sisters, guessing the position, asked her direct questions and were let into the secret. The numerous brothers, however, though they teased her about her poet, were less discerning and were kept in ignorance.

Elizabeth was in an agony of mind. She wanted – oh how she wanted – to marry Robert, but would she ever have courage to do it? She remembered vividly the awful thunderings of Edward Barrett when poor Henrietta had dared to love. She remembered Henrietta's tears and pleadings, how cruelly she was made to suffer, and how in utter despair she had meekly given up what had been her whole world. Could Elizabeth, so weak and dutiful, ever hope to succeed where her stronger sister had failed? Could her love for Robert overcome her fear of her father?

Winter became spring, the spring of 1846, when Henrietta became happily and furtively involved again – this time with Captain Surtees Cook, glorious and resplendent in his uniform of the guards. Robert Browning, with infinite patience, drew at length from Elizabeth a shaky agreement that their marriage should take place at the end of September. The summer presented many awkward moments because various relatives chose to visit the Barretts.

"I went to Elizabeth's room," declared one tactle

aunt, "and I saw a man there."

"Who is this Mr Browning who calls on Elizabeth so often?" asked another, and Mr Barrett himself, meeting Robert accidentally on the stairs demanded of his daughter,

"Has that man been with you *all day*, Elizabeth?" In spite of the strain of this sort of thing upon the invalid's nerves, the improvement in her health became apparent to all. She persevered with her walking and sometimes during carriage drives with Arabel she would alight in the park and wander quite a long way. She experienced then the strange, half-forgotten pleasure of feeling grass beneath her feet and of sitting under trees in the warm, fresh air. New life glowed in her pale cheeks and a new joy shone in her large, dark eyes. The dream of Italy drew nearer. The marriage time approached. August passed. September came.

Then on Thursday, September the tenth, there was a panic! Mr Barrett suddenly announced his intention of having the house decorated from floor to roof. He despatched George at once to seek a suitable seaside dence where the family could stay for a month or Elizabeth was in despair. Yet she clutched at ce of another delay. A month would bring e middle of October. The weather would be not wintry by then, and she would not be

172

able to undertake the journey abroad. Her letter to Browning telling the news brought a firm reply. He had been patient long enough.

"If you go with the family, our marriage will have to be postponed for a whole year," he wrote. "We must be married directly and go to Italy. I will go for a licence today and we can be married on Saturday." Saturday!

On Saturday morning at St Pancras Church, Marylebone, the two poets were married. Elizabeth was sadly alone except for Wilson, her trusted maid. She had not dared to tell even Henrietta and Arabel, for the less they knew, the less they could be blamed for any part in the plot. Browning took as witness only a cousin, James Silverthorne. Quietly the words were

spoken and the bond was forged. Elizabeth Barrett became Elizabeth Browning, but there was no relief in immediate flight. Plans had been carefully made, and for various reasons it was deemed advisable for Elizabeth to return home and remain there for one more week, leaving for Italy with her husband the following Saturday.

The strain of the secret marriage on one with so frail a body and tender a heart as Elizabeth must have been intense, but the week of deception afterwards came near to overwhelming her. It was no wonder that she jumped at every sound and read suspicion in every glance. It was impossible for her to join naturally in the family's excited talk about the approaching seaside holiday and she must have longed each day for night when she could feel and finger the wedding ring she was forced to hide.

Fortunately, there was much to be done. With Wilson's help, she had to pack and in view of the fact that everyone else was packing too, this was quite easy. Then, alone she had to face the bitter task of writing to her father asking pardon for seeking happiness (pardon that in his hardness he was never to give, just as later he was to refuse it to brother Alfred who married, and to Henrietta who ran away with Captain Cook). The luggage was somehow, at some time, secreted out of the house, and on Saturday afternoon, with Wilson and Flush, Elizabeth left. Long before, she had sadly described herself as a bird in a cage. Now the cage door was opened and the bird flew away.

Today, in Florence, Italy, there is a house with a tablet above the door,

"Here wrote and died Elizabeth Barrett Browning who, in her woman's heart, combined learning and poetry, and made of her verse a golden ring linking Italy and England. This memorial is placed by a grateful Florence, 1861."

Doctors had prescribed closed curtains and the four walls of one room for her. Over the years they had prophesied sudden death if she should undertake anything so hazardous as a tiring journey or force her frail body into anything like normal action. Yet she lived fifteen years after her elopement with Robert, fifteen years of happiness as perfect as any two people could ever hope to know.